The Legend of Ogopogo:
Canada's Loch Ness Monster

Jason Hewlett

The Legend of Ogopogo:
Canada's Loch Ness Monster

This edition published by Small Town Monsters Publishing, LLC in 2024

Author: Jason Hewlett

Cover Artist: Easton Hawk

Table of Contents

Foreword
On the Trail of Monsters
Eli Watson

I began my cryptozoological endeavors in 2018 with a podcast called *Cryptid Campfire*. I was working at a movie theater at the time, going to school to learn how to make films, and decided to create a podcast so that my friends and I could discuss Bigfoot and other cryptids. To me, the podcast was a creative outlet. A new medium of storytelling to explore outside of narrative films. Never would I have imagined back then that a 'hobby' like cryptozoology would end up changing my life in so many profound ways. Never in my wildest dreams would I have thought that a mere five years later I would be at Lake Okanagan in British Columbia, searching for Ogopogo. Yet, there I was in May of 2023, traveling by boat to Rattlesnake Island. What was so long just a name, or two words on a page, was now a real island in front of my eyes! This endeavor into Ogopogo was perhaps one of the most full-circle and surreal moments I've ever had the opportunity to experience, but to fully grasp it, I will have to share my story.

Picture the scene: October 18, 2018. Three of us are crammed in my grandmother's walk-in closet in Los Angeles, California. The podcast consisted of myself, Alex Daikaiju and Jasmine With. Alex had come over early to help me set up microphones, but we discovered that we did not have the proper cables. So, our set up extended into the time to record the episode, which for those unversed in the way of LA traffic, meant driving around town for three hours until we could find the right cables. Then, we finally returned to my grandmother's house to record THREE episodes. I almost thought Jasmine was going to quit before we even started. Did I mention that this was the first time we had ever met to record the podcast? It was awkward, and there was a lot of figuring out our dynamic as a trio, but we did it. We covered the Loch Ness Monster, Champ, and Ogopogo in one thirty-minute episode (not nearly giving each one their proper due). Feel free to listen to that whirlwind of an episode because that's how my foray into the world of cryptozoology began.

Fast forward a few years and I began to work with Nash Hoover on his series, *Chasing Legends*. There I met Aleksandar Petakov for the first time. We traveled the country, going to Vermont looking for Champ, the lake monster, and Louisiana, seeking evidence of the Rougarou. Through the connections I made working on this show, I was able to connect with Seth Breedlove, the Head Maestro of Small Town Monsters, a production company specializing in cryptid documentaries. From there I began to work with Small Town Monsters, and, in late 2022, I pitched a series that would follow myself as I explored phenomena that caught my interest. This series is known as *Mysteries & Monsters*. Like many shows that inspired me as a child like *MonsterQuest* or even shows that I thought were cool in my college years like *In Search Of*, I modeled my show to be a 'mystery of the week' deal. Every episode covers something different and while I follow up on certain research threads, a lot of my episodes follow different subjects in different parts of the country, which brings me back to Ogopogo.

Since its inception, this project has shifted forms until it settled into a full-length, stand-alone feature, which ultimately, I think it was meant to be. At the time however, planning this to be an episode of my series I knew I wanted to cover a story about a lake monster. Coincidentally, Seth was traveling to British Columbia to film another installment in his series *On the Trail of Bigfoot*, a project I would assist with, and I knew this was my chance to elevate my series to a new level and to pursue a mystery that genuinely interested me. I also knew that to pull the shoot off, I was going to need help from someone in British Columbia and, as it turned out, I knew a few.

Around the same time that I interviewed Seth Breedlove on *Cryptid Campfire*, I also interviewed a man named Jason Hewlett. I should honestly go back and listen to that episode because I can't even remember what I interviewed him about back then. That isn't a statement about the content of the episode, but rather a testament to the friendship that Jason and I have built up over the years. Jason and I have worked together in various ways in a short amount of time. In addition to appearing on my show multiple times, he was integral in bringing a video version of *Cryptid Campfire* to life on the *Paranormal Network* YouTube channel. Something that added a lot of exposure to me and the podcast as a whole.

My favorite part of working with Jason, however, is the fact that he reminds me a lot of myself. Jason and I are both obsessive workers. When we're involved with a project, we sink our teeth in and don't let go, even sometimes when it's to our detriment. We are also very loyal people. When we like someone, we do not let them go. We also have a lot of the same interests, obviously cryptids and the paranormal, but also, the movies we enjoy and even some of the same hobbies like building LEGO. Talking with Jason is a blast. He is approachable, knowledgeable, resourceful, and a fantastic logistical planner. I would even go so far as to say that without Jason, creating a documentary about Ogopogo would have been impossible. I was in a position where I needed someone to help me bring this documentary together, someone who knew the lay of the land, someone who was easy to work with, and there was no better fit for that than Jason.

I don't remember exactly when I approached Jason about the project, but I know that it was months in advance. I remember discussing the shoot for a long time. At some points, it felt like it was never going to happen because it was so far away. Then, when it finally came to the filming process, it went by quickly and incredibly smooth, and I can say that is a result of Jason's planning. I'm sure Jason will dive into all the details of the shoot in this book, but I have to say that what we accomplished in a few short days was truly a once-in-a-lifetime experience. From meeting Arlene Gaal's daughter, to riding to Rattlesnake Island with Bill Steciuk, and interviewing the people who took the most recent photograph of the lake creature, I couldn't have imagined a better shoot.

When I saw Lake Okanagan for the first time, I was driving up to Kelowna by myself in a rental car, and in that solitude, a feeling struck me like it has only a few times before in my life. It's a feeling that lets me know that no matter how strange or colorful and non-traditional my life is, I'm doing what I'm meant to do. I tried for years to make it in Hollywood, and when I stopped focusing on that and decided to learn more about something that was interesting to me (cryptozoology), it's like all the pieces came together and fell in my lap. The surreal feeling of realizing how serendipitous your whole life is, is bewildering. I've subscribed to this notion that we are not pushed forward by our previous actions but rather drawn forward by our ultimate destiny, and meeting Jason in Kelowna, after years of knowing each other online because I started a podcast for fun with my friends, felt like some aspect of my ultimate life journey fulfilled.

While I have not found the one magic piece of evidence that will convince a room full of skeptics that there is an undiscovered species in Lake Okanagan, I believe that Ogopogo is real. Almost everyone we interviewed had a sighting of the elusive lake dweller, and if they did not, they knew someone who did. These people come from all walks of life, with different beliefs, backgrounds, and outlooks, yet they all share this experience of seeing something in the lake. As I've investigated various cryptozoological cases in the past few years, I have run across many hoaxes or tall tales accentuated by Internet forums to the point where they exist in the subconscious of the masses. Some people will take those at face value and lump in outlandish and fictional creatures like the Snallygaster or Jackalope into the same category as Sasquatch or Ogopogo. The difference, however, is that there are thousands of witnesses of Sasquatch and Ogopogo, and that alone is rare. Combine witness testimony and trace evidence left behind that point to a real zoological possibility, and what you have is a true cryptozoological case.

Standing on the shores of Lake Okanagan, I felt a profound connection to the mystery. This is something real, that people are seeing and experiencing, and various aspects of my life had aligned to bring me there, to see the waters of the lake and talk to people who have seen it. Unlike other cryptids that rely on shoddy storytelling to remain relevant, Ogopogo is a mystery that endures because people continue to see it, and it will remain so as long as people see things they cannot explain in the lake. Without proper research and funding, we may never know what Ogopogo physically is, but the First Nations people, who were seeing Ogopogo long before the white man arrived, already have an answer: Ogopogo is the Spirit of the Lake. Once you've seen the lake, you've seen Ogopogo, so in one way I've seen it too. And if part of my ultimate destiny is to see a beautiful location like Lake Okanagan, well, I'm not complaining.

Mystery still exists in the world and fate works in mysterious ways. Not every corner of the map has been explored to the fullest. Not every creature is known to man. Don't let the status quo define what your eyes and ears perceive, because often the truth doesn't come neatly packaged. It often lies beneath the complex waves, sometimes clear, sometimes murky, sometimes calm, and sometimes turbulent, challenging you in ways that can frighten you, but I promise you, it's there. And if you find it, you may also find that you might be a different person than you were when you set out.

Introduction: Why Write a Book About Monsters?

During the summer of 1998, I found myself floating on a surfboard. I wasn't on the ocean, waiting to catch a wave. I was bobbing up and down on a lake in the Interior of British Columbia, catching some sun, no sign of a surfable wave in sight.

Growing up, my parents owned a cabin on Little Shuswap Lake, a small body of water connected via the appropriately named Little River to Shuswap Lake, which is about two hours northeast of Lake Okanagan. Lake Okanagan is, of course, home to the legendary monster known as Ogopogo, which has captivated mystery and monster fans for generations and become a tourism mascot for the region.

Being free-range children, my friends and I spent a great deal of time down on the beach, swimming in the lake, and hanging out on the dock. Spending my youth this way, it created a lifelong love of being on, in, or near the water. To this day, I feel more at home near a body of water than pretty much anywhere else.

My friends and I heard the stories of Ogopogo – you couldn't grow up in the region and not – and many of us were fascinated by them. Our conversations included theories about what Ogopogo could be, why it existed, what it ate, and, more ominously to our young minds, could it find its way to our lake via some elaborate underground tunnel system?

Little did we know that Shuswap Lake, which was just one little river away, is rumored to contain its own lake monster: the Shuswaggi – a twenty-five-foot-long serpentine cousin of Ogopogo. Had we known this at the time, we'd have probably been less likely to spend our time pondering such things.

But we did, and these discussions turned to dares from time to time. My dad had built a floating dock anchored some ways from shore, one that could be moved deeper as the lake's depth decreased throughout the summer. One of our favorite dares was to move the floating dock as far out as the anchor chain would allow, swim out at sunset, talk about Ogopogo, and then swim back once it was dark.

This might not sound like much of a dare, but once our young imaginations got the better of us, that swim to shore could be downright terrifying! On more than one occasion, it wouldn't be unusual for one of us to quietly slip beneath the surface, swim to the other, and tug on their feet.

I know, we were jerks.

This created a kind of healthy, thrilling fear of whatever could possibly live beneath the surface of both the lake I grew up on and any lake in general, which brings me back to that hot summer day in 1998. I was twenty-six at the time, and alone at the family cabin, having just returned from a year-long adventure in Australia. I needed time to think, recover from the severe jet lag I felt, and ponder my next move in life. The furthest thing from my mind was Ogopogo or any other lake monster.

Seated upright on the board, my legs dangling in the water, I let my mind wander and my gaze soften, the bright sun making that easy as it reflected off the lake with an almost blinding intensity.

Then something moved beneath the surfboard and brushed the bottom of my foot!

What I likely saw swim below me was a trick of the mind created by the sparkling sunlight on the water and my soft gaze. What brushed my foot could have been a fish, or, more likely, a bit of seaweed as the low water meant the weeds weren't that deep at this point in the summer.

But my mind immediately flashed back to my youth, the hours spent talking lake monsters with my friends, and those dares we made to each on those hot summer nights. For an instant I was terrified something was in the lake and it had just swum underneath me.

If you've read the previous books I've written with my colleague Peter Renn, *I Want to Believe: One Man's Journey into the Paranormal*, *I Want to Believe: An Investigators' Archive*, and *Dying Light: An Investigation into Near-Death Experiences*, you know I've had a lifelong interest in the unexplained and spend a good deal of my time researching and investigating ghosts, hauntings and other high strangeness as a part of the Canadian Paranormal Society, a group Peter and I co-founded in 2020. While we have ventured into the woods in search of Bigfoot, we haven't dedicated much time in search of the elusive Ogopogo for a variety of reasons.

The biggest hurdle to an Ogopogo investigation, or any lake-monster expedition for that matter, is the fact these creatures exist in a lake. Lakes can be huge and, unless you have a lot of money at your disposal to bankroll a full-on search, your efforts are reduced to observing from shore. Given the amount of ground these lakes can cover, it makes spotting an elusive creature akin to finding the proverbial needle in a haystack.

Another reason for our lack of effort is my general belief that, of all the monsters out there, Ogopogo and his like seem the least likely to exist. As big as a lake can get, it still takes up a finite amount of space and has a defined depth. If something as big as an Ogopogo or a Loch Ness Monster really lived in one, I believe sightings would be more frequent. This is especially true given the duration of which these monsters have been sighted.

When it comes to Ogopogo, sightings date back hundreds of years. There would need to be a large enough population of this species to support its reproduction over the centuries. Again, if this was the case, you'd think there would be more sightings, and even more than a few carcasses found both in the lake and on shore.

Despite my skepticism, I still find the idea of lake monsters enticing. As with most aspects of the paranormal, I want these creatures to exist. The possibility they might, no matter how remote, makes the world a far more interesting place to live in. I'm clearly not the only one to feel this way.

Municipalities in the Okanagan have embraced the idea of Ogopogo and turned it into a tourism mascot, as have other regions around the world where such creatures are believed to exist.

Ogopogo's origin dates to the region's original Indigenous tribes, and as often happens with Sasquatch, the legend is an important part of the people's culture which is still celebrated today.

When a photograph of an alleged Ogopogo surfaced in the fall of 2022, it went viral and renewed interest in the story. The photograph, taken by Dale Hanchar and Colleen Hanson, depicts what could be the mythological beast resting just beneath the lake's surface. Skeptics have said it looks like a bird or even a wolf. Regardless, the picture made international news, as such sightings tend to do, proving the public remains very much fascinated by the Ogopogo and creatures like it.

It sparked a renewed interest in me as well. Whatever Hanchar and Hanson took a picture of – and you'll hear their account later in this book – there was something in the lake that day. Is it the same something people have reported for hundreds of years? If people aren't seeing a monster, what variety of phenomena is keeping the story alive?

This is what I'm attempting to answer with this book. In addition to various witness stories, I've gathered a collection of believers and skeptics, in addition to speaking with someone from the local Indigenous community, in an effort to find answers. As I have with my previous books,

I'll leave it up to you, the reader, to decide for yourselves in the end.

The writing of this book also coincides with an expedition by my friend and fellow paranormal enthusiast, Eli Watson. Eli is a part of the Small Town Monsters independent production company, which documents stories about monsters all over North America. Eli travelled to British Columbia in the spring of 2023 and invited me to join him in his quest to find evidence of Ogopogo. I've documented our adventures – and any findings – in this book.

Regardless of my thoughts, and any evidence to support or deny the creature's existence, the story of Ogopogo and his cousins worldwide is a fascinating and entertaining one.

In the end, I think people just like a good monster story; something to talk about around a campfire or to keep us up at night. I hope this book contributes to this enjoyment in some way.

To begin, let's start with an overview of what people might be seeing out there. To kick us off, I've turned to a man who knows a thing or two about monsters, cryptozoologist Ken Gerhard.

Here There Be Monsters

When Ken Gerhard was a young boy, he thought he saw a lake monster.

His family lived in Minnesota at the time, and there was a small lake behind his home. He was eight or nine years old and hanging out in his backyard staring at the lake. To this day, Gerhard swears he saw a hump rise out of the water – a classic hump like the one many people associate with the Loch Ness Monster.

He's not sure how long the hump rested on the surface, but Gerhard was aware enough to know there weren't any boats or other objects on the lake he could mistake for the hump that could cause a wake to create such a form. The hump eventually sunk back beneath the surface, and Gerhard was left wondering what the heck he just saw.

Already fascinated by Bigfoot, this encounter fuelled a passion that eventually led Gerhard to study cryptozoology and make it his life's work. Cryptozoology is a pseudoscience that searches for and studies unknown, legendary, or extinct animals whose current existence can be disputed or unsubstantiated. Such animals include Bigfoot, the Loch Ness Monster, the Jersey Devil, and, naturally, Ogopogo.

Gerhard's work has made him a prominent figure in the cryptozoology subculture and led to appearances on such television programs as *In Search of Monsters*, *The UnXplained*, *The Proof is Out There* and documentaries like *Terror in the Skies* and *Searching for Sasquatch 4: Eyes in the Night*. He's also written several books on the subject, including *The Essential Guide to the Loch Ness Monster and other Aquatic Cryptids*.

We met while Gerhard was promoting that book, and he appeared on my award-winning YouTube series *We Want to Believe* during episodes where we went in search of Sasquatch. He was one of the first people I turned to for knowledge when I decided to write this book, and what follows is a transcription of an interview I conducted with him via Zoom.

Gerhard has investigated Loch Ness personally, as well as other lake monsters around the world, but he has yet to explore Lake Okanagan, a task which is on his To-Do List. He says the location, and the story of Ogopogo, is a mecca for cryptozoologists.

He is well aware of Ogopogo, though, having heard stories about the creature back in the 1970s when he was initially interested in the subject of lake monsters and wild men of the forests.

"In fact, I probably first heard about it on the TV show *In Search Of* in the late 70s. They did an episode, and I know there was a book out at that time by an author named Mary Moon. I have a copy of that, and it was one of the first books that ever came out (about Ogopogo).

"Through the years I've caught TV shows, and I've read all of Arlene Gaal's books. John Kirk is a good friend of mine, and, of course, he's spent a lot of time researching there. So, I've got bits and pieces of information from different sources."

Indeed, Moon's book was published in 1977 and has the lofty title *Ogopogo: The Okanagan Mystery from Indian Lore to Contemporary Evidence, The Facts About the Legendary Monster of British Columbia's Okanagan Lake*.

Arlene Gaal, who died in late 2021 at the age of eighty-four, wrote three books on Ogopogo including *In Search of Ogopogo: Sacred Creature of the Okanagan* and *Ogopogo: The True Story of the Okanagan Lake Million Dollar Monster*. She was considered one of the world's leading Ogopogo researchers and was often contacted by people who believed they'd seen the beast. She also consulted on many television shows that came to Kelowna to report on Ogopogo: programs like *Unsolved Mysteries* and the aforementioned *In Search Of*.

John Kirk is a cryptozoologist and chairman of the British Columbia Scientific Cryptozoology Club and the author of *In the Domain of Lake Monsters*. He also has a book on Ogopogo in the works.

While Gerhard might not be an expert *per se* on Ogopogo, he has enough knowledge to say with confidence that what people believe they are seeing fits into the paradigm of the worldwide lake monster phenomenon. This includes sightings of creatures in Loch Ness, Lake Champlain, and various other lakes around the world. In fact, lake monsters are reported everywhere, from Japan to Iceland and Ireland to Russia.

What people are seeing – or believe they are seeing – are creatures with striking similarities despite there being vast geographical distances between them. Gerhard also says the habitats these creatures are seen in – the lakes – have enough similarities to make these sightings compelling.

Ogopogo is considered one of the most widely seen and reported lake monsters on record. In fact, Gerhard explains the creature has been witnessed more than once by multiple people at the same time.

"There have been a couple of accounts (of Ogopogo) that have involved a large number of eyewitnesses, fifteen to seventeen eyewitnesses at the same time, and I think those would go back to the 1950s or 60s. So, it has been observed by a lot of people, or at least it has been in the past."

More recent sightings have taken place in 2019 and 2022, with the reports made by one or two people at a time.

One of the more compelling bits of video evidence, if not the most compelling, was filmed by Blake Neudorf in July of 2018, says Gerhard. The video didn't surface, if you'll pardon the pun, until early 2020. It clearly shows what looks like a serpentine form swimming along the lake's surface with a caterpillar-like motion. The water is relatively calm and void of any signs of a boat wake.

Gerhard reviewed the footage on the television series *The Proof is Out There* and believes what Neudorf captured was evidence of an animal swimming across the lake.

"A marine biologist that they had on the show actually confirmed that it was a living animal, in her opinion. In recent years, that's a pretty good piece of evidence."

The serpentine description is very much in line with what people have seen in Lake Okanagan and other lakes around the world believed to be home to monsters. This even holds true of Loch Ness despite the popular belief that Nessie could be a Plesiosaurus, a long extinct type of aquatic dinosaur.

According to witness accounts, and Gerhard's own research, the creature that people describe seeing in Loch Ness pretty much fits the exact description of Ogopogo, Champ, and other lake monsters.

"And remember most people see it just breaking the surface of the lake. It's what can actually be seen and not the parts below the surface of the lake."

With that in mind, the archetype for Ogopogo, Nessie, and their ilk is anywhere from twelve to forty feet in length with a very snake-like form, black, brown, or grey in color with shiny skin. Those who have seen the head describe it as being horse-like or sheep-like while the tail is that of a whale.

The Plesiosaurus description didn't become popular until the famed – and eventually proven as a hoax – Surgeon's Photograph of Nessie taken in 1934.

"Everyone has seen that photo. It's been in every book and TV show," Gerhard continues.

On April 21, 1934, the *Daily Mail* in the United Kingdom published this photograph, arguably the most famous picture taken of the monster. It was reportedly taken by a doctor named Robert Kenneth Wilson and depicts the now trademark long neck of Nessie emerging from the rippling waters of Loch Ness. Sixty years later, in 1994, Christopher Spurling verified the picture was a fake.

Spurling, the stepson of famed big-game hunter Marmaduke Wetherell, explained that Wetherell enlisted his help to create the monster's neck and place it on a toy submarine. Wilson was selected to give the photograph to the media because of his trusted reputation as a doctor.

Why go to all this trouble? Wetherell was hired by the *Daily Mail* in 1933 to find proof of the Loch Ness Monster's existence. He returned from his expedition with evidence of large footprints leading from the lake's shore into the water. However, researchers with the Natural History Museum concluded the track had been made with a dried hippo's foot, humiliating Wetherell. One can conclude hoaxing the Surgeon's Photograph was an ill-fated way to get back at those who doubted his reputation.

There were early, land-based sightings of a monster at Loch Ness which fit the Plesiosaurus description, but Gerhard believes those were misidentification or hoaxes themselves.

Gerhard estimates about eighty-five percent of Loch Ness sightings are only of the humps of an unidentified species as they move through the surface of the water, which suggests a snake-like form and not a solid, large body. He says this is true of most Ogopogo witnesses as well.

"When it undulates, or swims up and down, it creates these loops or humps on the surface of the water, and that's what's been described in regard to lake monsters all over the world, including Nessie.

"I think that whatever is in Lake Okanagan is very likely the same species that we're finding in Loch Ness and other lakes around the world in the Northern Hemisphere, and possibly in the ocean from time to time."

Indeed, there is an old seafarer's tradition of serpent-like monsters being spotted in the world's oceans dating back to when humans first started travelling across them. In fact, there've been several sightings off the coast of Western Canada of just such a beast, which locals call Cadborosaurus.

The Cadborosaurus, or Caddy as the alleged beast is affectionately called, has been spotted for more than a hundred years along the Western Coast of North America, from the coastline of British Columbia south to Washington State. The Salish First Nations of British Columbia drew petroglyphs of the monster, depicting a long creature with a dragon-like head. Sightings by settlers date back to the late 1800s but Caddy gained everlasting fame when the monster first appeared on the front page of the *Victoria Times Colonist* in 1933.

That encounter had Caddy spotted near Chatham Island in Cadboro Bay on Vancouver Island, with a witness reporting a long, dark green creature as large as a whale appearing with a snort and a hiss. Caddy has been seen in that location many more times since then.

Given the similar descriptions and proximity to Lake Okanagan, Gerhard believes there's a chance Caddy and

Ogopogo are the same species. The Columbia River does connect Lake Okanagan to the Pacific Ocean, albeit tenuously, so there's also a chance such a creature could travel back and forth from the lake to the ocean, he says.

"I think Cadborosaurus is the same thing as the Loch Ness Monster and what's in Lake Okanagan.

"It's much easier from a scientific standpoint to make the argument that there's one remarkable unknown species that explains all of these accounts worldwide as opposed to different types… That just seems more probable, especially when the eyewitness descriptions and habitats are so similar."

Another collaborating piece of evidence to support these creatures' existence is indeed the habitats in which they live. Gerhard has studied the various lakes where sightings take place and has found many similarities between them.

Lake Okanagan is a long, narrow lake like Loch Ness. Both were carved out at the end of the Pleistocene era by glaciers, making them glacial lakes. The lakes were likely on a geographical rift, were widened as the glaciers retreated, and then filled with water during the melt, he says.

Loch Ness is twenty-two-and-a-half miles long and just shy of two miles wide. Lake Okanagan is about eighty-four miles long and three miles wide. While Lake Okanagan is the bigger lake, both are of a similar depth, with Loch Ness measured at seven hundred and fifty-four feet at its greatest depth and Lake Okanagan seven hundred and sixty-one feet. Gerhard's research shows the water temperatures are also similar in the two, although there's greater temperature fluctuation in Lake Okanagan. In Loch Ness the deepest water maintains an average temperature of forty-two degrees Fahrenheit year-round while Lake Okanagan maintains about forty-five degrees Fahrenheit.

"Also, the types of fish that inhabit both lakes are primarily salmonid types of fishes like kokanee, trout, and salmon. Things like that which, theoretically, is a food type for these animals if they're carnivores."

Both lakes are also in what cryptozoologists call the Lake Monster Belt at about forty to sixty degrees north latitude. Gerhard says Lake Okanagan and Loch Ness are only separated by about eight degrees of latitude.

Why call it the Lake Monster Belt? Gerhard said most lakes with monster sightings rest within these geographical latitudes, from Canada to Europe. Many of these lakes are the same in terms of structure, water depth, temperature, and food source.

"All these lakes are kind of in the same belt. They were all formed about the same time period at the end of the Pleistocine about ten or twelve thousand years ago. They are all very cold, deep lakes with a similar type of fish population. That, as a cryptozoologist, to me is very interesting."

So, what are these lake monsters that people are seeing? Are they simply an animal that has not been identified or are they evolved from a previously discovered species? Gerhard believes many sightings are misidentification of other fish, natural phenomena like wave effects, and even hoaxes. But a case can be made that other sightings are likely that of a still unidentified species.

"I don't necessarily think that every single account out there of an unknown lake monster is one hundred percent accurate, but I think you could make a case that there is a remarkable unknown species."

If there is a monster in Lake Okanagan, it's not a reptile because reptiles do not adapt to cold-water environments, says Gerhard. Nor is he convinced it's a fish, which many skeptics credit the sightings to, especially eels. He points out eels do not have humps, which are reported in almost every lake monster sighting.

The humps and swimming up and down motion people believe they see speak to something mammalian, like a whale, Gerhard emphasizes. In his book *The Essential Guide to the Loch Ness Monster and Other Aquatic Cryptids*, Gerhard resurrected an older hypothesis that Nessie – and other potential lake monsters – are a prehistoric type of whale known as a Basilosaurus or Archosaur, which roamed the planet twenty to forty million years ago. Both were mammals with a snake-like form.

"That's what some witnesses of Ogopogo have described it as: a snaky whale," he says.

Whales are warm-blooded species that adapt well to cold-water environments. They also swim with an up-and-down motion in line with what witnesses to lake monster sightings describe. They also have the smooth skin and the two-pronged horizontal tails some people have reported as well.

"And the head as being horse like. That's interesting too," continues Gerhard. "If you look at reconstructions of Archosaurs and Basilosaurus they had a very horse-shaped head. The teeth were much sharper and pointier because they were carnivores, but one who saw a head sticking out of the water could very easily interpret that as being horse like, in my opinion."

If these creatures exist, a whale offshoot would also have a much easier time of moving inland via rivers than a fish species because they are air breathers, he reveals.

If not a mammal, Gerhard believes a species of amphibian could also be responsible for the sightings. Amphibians adapt to cold water better than reptiles despite being a cold-blooded species and can breathe through their skin while underwater. This could explain why the creatures are not seen more often.

"Regardless of what category we want to put it in, it would make sense that it would be a prehistoric species because things got a lot bigger back then" he claims. "Some of the accounts kind of reference those."

Another commonality between all these alleged monsters is a strong connection to local folklore and Indigenous peoples, much like the connection between Sasquatch and native North Americans. Gerhard says this is especially true with Ogopogo, or *N'ha-a-itk* as the creature is named by the people of the Westbank First Nations.

We'll dive deeper into the Westbank First Nations relationship with *N'ha-a-itk* in a future chapter, but Gerhard's research revealed *N'ha-a-itk* is historically believed to have lived near Rattlesnake Island at Squally Point on the southern part of Lake Okanagan.

"It was basically a guardian or demon of the lake and there had to be a sacrifice or toll paid, if you will, if you wanted to traverse the lake. Often it was said that natives would take a dog or chicken or a pig and heave it into the water as a sacrifice to *N'ha-a-itk* so they wouldn't get screwed with."

This story is like First Nation legends Gerhard heard while researching in Alaska, where Indigenous people of the Knik Tribe spoke of a similar ritual to the Iliamna Monster, *Jig-ik-nak*. He says there are great native traditions across North America of great horned serpents inhabiting various lakes as well.

Cryptozoology is very much a mosaic of different types of research with zoology and folklore being at the forefront. He says when you have these enduring First Nations traditions and a lot of modern sightings of something similar, the similarities cannot, nor should not, be ignored.

"You've got to pay attention to that. That's another layer of evidence that something has been there for a long time," believes Gerhard.

But what about the lack of proof? If these stories have persisted for hundreds of years, why hasn't a body washed up on the shore of one of these lakes? And why aren't there more sightings of these monsters? Will we ever get answers to these questions? Gerhard tries to remain optimistic on this one.

Based on his own research, investigating lake monster sightings is logistically more challenging than venturing into the woods to look for Sasquatch. You're looking for something underwater, often in bodies of water with great depths, and the equipment used to look for these alleged creatures – like side-scan sonar – is very expensive.

That being said, there's been some success in picking up sound anomalies using underwater listening devices like hydrophones, including whale-like communication in the depths of Lake Champlain. Gerhard said sonar readings have also picked up something within Loch Ness.

"There have probably been some (sonar contacts) in Lake Okanagan but not as many as in other lakes," he states.

The best chance cryptozoologists have of proving the existence of these creatures, other than finding a corpse or partial skeleton, is the use of Environmental DNA or eDNA. Environmental DNA originates from cellular material shed by organisms into aquatic or terrestrial environments. These can then be sampled and monitored using new molecular methods.

Dr. Neil Gemmell of the University of Otago in New Zealand did an eDNA study at Loch Ness between 2018 and 2019, taking two hundred and fifty water samples from around the Loch at different locations and depths. Once all the biological material was filtered out of the water, samples of some two thousand living aquatic species were identified.

Gemmell ruled out any chance of a prehistoric monster living in the lake and found no evidence of catfish, sturgeon or even shark DNA. He did, however, find a significant amount of eel DNA, supporting the popular theory that Nessie sightings could be the result of a giant eel.

Gerhard said an Environmental DNA test could provide answers to the Lake Okanagan mystery.

"Of course, as a cryptozoologist, you're always hoping for that home run, which would really be a carcass or at least a bone, tooth or significant part of a carcass that you could present to scientists, and they wouldn't be able to deny that here is something that we don't currently have documented in zoology. Hopefully that will happen."

Although I doubt that will ever happen, I share Gerhard's enthusiasm as someone who would also love for these mythical creatures to be real in some way, shape, or form. Which begged one final question: why does our fascination for these monsters endure despite the lack of good, hard evidence?

Gerhard believes it's because all people love and yearn for mystery, adventure, and exploration in their lives, adding it keeps life from getting too mundane and boring.

"The thought that there are things out there to conquer, conquests if you will, and great discoveries to be made. It certainly excites me."

Monsters have been with us for thousands of years and have many different symbolic meanings depending on the culture that fostered them. Gerhard says a lot of the lake monster stories mimic dragon legends from around the world. This is true with Nessie and its alleged relationship to Urquhart Castle.

Dragons date back four thousand years to ancient Babylon and Tiamat – antagonist to the hero Marduk, Gerhard explains.

"Tiamat is depicted as a serpent-like dragon from the sea, with impenetrable scales, sharp talons, and pointy horns – the personification of chaos. A thousand years later, the Old Testament mentions Leviathan – a great, aquatic serpent 300 miles long, possessing of mighty fins, sporting frightening teeth and a body covered in double-plated armor. In Norse Viking mythology, the Midgard Serpent – Jormungandr – dwells in the sea where it encircles the globe, perpetually grasping the end of its own tail with its mighty jaws."

There's also been a long-standing tradition of seafaring monsters inspired by the mysteries and associated fears early explorers had of great depths. For centuries, starting when people first started traveling by sea in those great ships, sailors would come back after months of exploring and regale people with tales of all kinds of adventures. Sometimes these stories involved sea monsters.

"I think that's always been a fascination for people; what great beasts are there hidden in the oceans and waterways of the world?" muses Gerhard. "The oceans kind of have that foreboding sense of mystery because we can't see what's really down there."

In fact, there was a fifteenth century Swedish map maker named Olaus Magnus who made ocean maps that included images of sea monsters swallowing whole ships. As well the Hunt-Lenox Globe, which was constructed in

1510 and is one of the first European globes ever made, containing the famous warning *hic sunt dracones* – Latin for *here be dragons* – on the southeast coast of Asia.

"That was a thing back in the day, too. You didn't want to go too far out because one of these mysterious monsters, whether it was a Kraken or great sea serpent, might swallow your ship whole."

I've always appreciated Gerhard's insight into the cryptid phenomenon. After speaking with him, I now feel I have a better and modern understanding of what many believe could be out there lurking in these lakes as well as why our society is fascinated with them.

Before venturing further, I thought it best to take a step back and talk to someone who isn't so sure these creatures exist, although he'd love it if they did. That person is skeptic Daniel Loxton.

Why There Aren't Monsters

For whatever reason, the term skeptic is taboo in the modern world of paranormal investigation. Ditto the idea of being skeptical of any reports of paranormal activity. It seems, at least from my experience, that those with a vested interest in the subject want people to take every report, sighting, and experience at face value: that something paranormal has happened. But shouldn't those of us who believe in the paranormal, or at the very least who want to believe in it, have a healthy level of skepticism?

To be skeptical, or display skepticism, is to have an attitude of doubt or some reservation about something. That's all. If you're skeptical, you aren't willing to believe anything outright. You want proof in the form of good, hard evidence. Think Occam's Razor, which is a philosophical tool for "shaving off" unlikely explanations. Once all possibilities are exhausted, the simplest explanation is likely the correct one, but you've got to remove all other possibilities first.

Yes, this means an investigator will quite often debunk events that many think are paranormal. Those ghostly footsteps are likely the house settling or the furnace vents causing the floorboards to shift. But once those possibilities are ruled out, and the phenomena persists, you just might have something otherworldly going on.

As a result, I think a healthy dose of skepticism is important in this line of work, and skeptical people are important to include among your ghost or monster hunting team. Some readers will likely bristle at the notion as – and let's be completely honest here – many skeptics can be downright hostile towards believers.

Case in point is the response I received from a university professor I approached via email as a potential interviewee for this book. He replied, and I quote:

"Your lack of a formal education seems to have served you well, as you don't know enough to understand how deeply flawed your ideas are. That must be a comfort to you, as you occupy the mind space of a three-year-old."

[I have a high-school degree, a diploma in film studies and a Bachelor of Journalism, plus spent a decade as a crime reporter for a major daily newspaper. For the record.]

Attitudes like that are what pit the skeptical against the believer, and vice versa. This is a shame, as balancing an open mind with a healthy dose of skepticism and realism is a far better approach to life in general.

What the world needs is more people like Daniel Loxton.

Loxton is a Canadian writer, illustrator, and skeptical researcher who has written dozens of critical thinking articles for the likes of *eSkeptic*, *Skeptic Magazine* and the *Skeptical Inquirer*, among many others. He's also penned a half dozen books that cast a skeptical eye on the possible existence of Bigfoot, the Loch Ness Monster, and other paranormal phenomena.

He's been in the field of scientific skepticism and misinformation research for the better part of two decades, a journey that began when he was a boy. Like me, Indiana Jones was his hero, and those cinematic adventures opened the young Loxton to the possibility that strange and supernatural things could exist alongside our rational world. Also, like me, he consumed every book and TV show about the paranormal and was especially drawn to cryptids like Bigfoot and the Loch Ness Monster.

"That's what got me involved in skepticism. I had a deep love for these stories," said Loxton.

When it comes to the story of Ogopogo, Loxton pointed out he is not a domain expert on the subject; although, he is well read on the topic. At one point he hefted an armload of books he's read on the material, including the works of Arlene Gaal. He's also done some of his own research on Ogopogo within the larger context of lake monsters, having written extensively on the likelihood – or not – that the Loch Ness Monster exists. This research has also extended into the realm of sea monsters like Cadborosaurs.

"I have a good, general cryptozoological background on the topic and some specific knowledge of Ogopogo," he said.

Diving in, Loxton said the conversation I had with Coralee Miller about Ogopogo's cultural significance (more on that later) is one of the most interesting things about the creature's narrative, saying it has a genuine and complicated origin story in First Nations lore. This includes the recent copyright debate between the Indigenous population and the City of Vernon, which we'll also discuss in an upcoming chapter. This is not to mention how Ogopogo itself has been a part of the non-native community's legacy for more than a century. The community has a deep fondness for the story.

This comes with more complicated questions about the fidelity of the First Nations lore as well as decolonization questions about what Western society has done to these stories by turning them into a tourist attraction. Loxton poses the question if this is a correctable wrong.

"To what extent are there complicated feedback loops too? The people alive now who are working to retrieve their languages and stories, they are not pre-Columbian people. They are people with televisions. They watch the paranormal shows that play on APTN. So, these stories and how they can be disentangled at this point in history is a really good question."

At this, Loxton and I shared stories about how, as children, we'd visit the Ogopogo statue while visiting Kelowna, hang from it and have our pictures taken. As adults we've taken our own children to this very same statue and had them pose for pictures while sharing what we know of the legend with them. This speaks to Ogopogo's enduring presence in our culture as well, and how the story continues to be passed on from generation to generation.

Before getting to the elephant-in-the-room question of whether Loxton believes Ogopogo/*N'ha-a-itk* is real, I asked him why he thinks stories like this endure in Western culture, especially in an age of science and reason. Why is there still a desire to believe in something like an Ogopogo?

Loxton believes humans have three major domains that define our existence – the practical, material and natural domain we can address with science and technology, the religious domain that addresses matters of the spirit, afterlife and ultimate meaning, and the third domain, which is beyond our range of knowledge and sight, but not beyond our control.

"I think those are just built into the human psyche," he said.

When the scientific skepticism movement began in the 1970s, and the likes of Isaac Asimov, Carl Sagan, and James Randy started taking a good, hard look at this unexplainable phenomena, there was an expectation that they would work out the fact behind it and explain it to people in a rational way that would close the book on the existence of ghosts, UFOs, and monsters like Bigfoot and Ogopogo. But that hasn't happened, and Loxton believes it never will.

"There will be people on Mars one day taking some kind of questionable substance while experiencing visitations from ghosts and having psychic premonitions. That will always be part of our being. It's a built-in part of the human condition. It seems to be part of how we interact with the world."

Water monsters have a significant storytelling value, often taking on the form of a cautionary tale. Loxton says these stories explore the mysteries of the sea, as there's far more to the world's bodies of water than can be seen with the naked eye.

"It's its own invisible world where anything can exist."

There's also a current movement, at least in the province of British Columbia where Ogopogo is said to live, where there's an obligation for people to be caretakers of the environment and respectful to the natural elements: elements like water where these creatures are rumored to reside. This factors into the story of Ogopogo, he says.

You'll learn more about this when we talk to the Westbank First Nations later in the book, but Loxton said Western culture has spun this folklore to present a more fearsome creature while First Nations believe it a more beloved kind of being. His research suggests the "sacrifices" made to Ogopogo were more akin to sage and tobacco than dead animals and the like.

Such twisting of tales is a very Western thing to do. Almost like we want to present the scariest story imaginable, probably because it sells better than something benign. I think this comes from a lack of understanding of the source material… and greed, of course.

This cultural misappropriation comes with Sasquatch as well. Loxton said every Indigenous community has its Wildman story, but not all these stories are the same. He describes it as a cluster of storytelling with some of these tales getting downright weird. In some, Sasquatch has a long pointy toe it uses to kill people with while in another it lives underwater.

"Even within a region, even within the most authentic versions of those stories that have existed since contact, there is diversity in the stories. That's hard for us to tease out at this point in history and especially with us being settlers."

When it comes to the paranormal, our belief in and fascination with the subject is often borne out of a desire to understand why we're here in the first place and what happens when we die, says Loxton. We want explanations for the things that befall us in life and to get more meaning out of our lives.

An example is the emergence of the witch hunting craze in Europe in the 1800s. He says this emerged out of a desire to improve science when the practice of human health started to show cracks in the system, so to speak.

"There were just things that went on with human health that weren't easily explained within the existing theoretical framework. Once you start noticing that there's that eureka moment where 'That's weird. How do we explain that?' It's a core scientific impulse but it actually opens a space then for other explanatory stories."

Those "eureka moments" didn't fit into the popular medical and scientific theory of the day so they were deemed as interference from witches, Loxton explains. Leaps to the paranormal were used to try and explain why a variety of difficult-at-the-time concepts such as why children would go missing or even the rising and setting of the sun.

He believes the modern fascination with and focus on conspiracy theories is a modern example of this feral critical thinking, as it were.

"They're asking a lot of questions and seeking answers but in a way that's untethered from evidence. It's not enough to think carefully about it. At some point you have to be tied to some body of evidence to keep you from going down the rabbit hole altogether."

Taking it back to lake monsters then, what is it people are seeing – or think they're seeing – out on the water? Loxton believes there's a tendency by both proponents of cryptozoology and skeptics to pick what he calls a "neat explanation" to explain a series of unexplainable events. These explanations range from monsters to otters when, in fact, the truth could be any number of things.

Loxton knows of the hundreds, if not thousands, of lakes reported to be haunted by some kind of monster. It is clear people are seeing something in the water, but until it's proven that there's a monster in these lakes, Loxton asserts that the odds are they are seeing something else. Or, perhaps more accurately, a bunch of somethings.

He uses sleep paralysis as an example. When people have a terrifying experience like that and don't know where it came from, they tend to look for some culturally available template to fit that experience into. Hence some people interpret the encounter as being attacked by a ghost or an alien abduction or even demonic spiritual warfare.

"Once they make that connection, they tend to strengthen it over time with retellings (of the experience) and so on.

"Monsters are a culturally available template for ambiguous things seen in certain places. I'm certain lots of lake monster sightings have been otters. Lots of sea serpent sightings have been seals or sea lions or that kind of thing. Lots of Bigfoot sightings have been bears."

Loxton used to herd sheep and during that time he saw a lot of bears. He also saw a lot of stump bears, meaning tree stumps that looked like bears. Especially the burnt stumps, which had a myriad of shades and dark colors.

"A lot of them your brain turns into bears. And at least in one case we spent a few minutes looking at a Sasquatch as it stood there in broad daylight and stared at us. It's only when we got a better look at that tree stump from another angle that the illusion broke down. But it was really compelling. We could almost see it moving its head."

Loxton's point is valid. Many Bigfoot sightings can be attributed to bears, which can walk upright for short periods of time, and stumps, especially burnt stumps. My Canadian Paranormal Society colleague Olivier Asselin, who you'll meet later in this book, took a picture of such a Stumpsquatch, and it was so convincing it even fooled my skeptical wife.

If such tricks of the eye happen with Bigfoot, then it most definitely happens with lake monsters. Loxton takes Loch Ness as an example, using the Dinsdale Film to make a point.

During the spring of 1960 Tim Dinsdale, an aeronautical engineer, ventured to Loch Ness on a quest to prove the existence of the elusive creature. He indeed captured on film what many believe is the first ever footage of Nessie; a grainy black and white close-up of what looks like a large animal swimming along the surface of the lake.

Many believe that bit of film to be the only footage Dinsdale shot during his trip, but Loxton says the one made public was the last bit of film he recorded. The other footage Dinsdale filmed ended up being misidentified birds, then a rock, and then a log.

"And then whatever is in that last film, which could be a monster or boat," explains Loxton.

Loxton says John Kirk, who you will also meet later in this book, recounts misidentification cases in his book on Ogopogo, adding that happens a lot when one goes in search of monsters.

There are also sightings that are difficult to explain as misidentifications. Kirk's book contains some "spectacular examples" such as full arches out of the water in Lake Okanagan, which Loxton admits is difficult to explain away.

"We have those in our first-person experience sometimes. 'What the heck was that?'," he continues.

"Those stories are recounted to the public in literature, and, as an outsider, who can determine if what the person saw was a Bigfoot or lake monsters, made up the story entirely, or perhaps the person telling the story is crazy... I don't know as an outsider. I have to make some kind of assessment about that. Often all you can do is throw up your hands."

What we as consumers of such tales can do is dig deeper into the literature and folklore and see if there are other similar accounts, including by the witness, he clarifies. One can even further research the witness to learn more about him or her and see how reliable a witness they are.

He used Albert Ostman's famous Bigfoot encounter as an example. The Canadian prospector claims he was abducted by Sasquatch in 1924 and held captive for about a week before he could trick the family of ape-like creatures and escape. It's the type of story that's become legendary in the cryptozoology field.

Loxton has done his due diligence and dug deeper into Ostman's past, finding an earlier telling of the story by Ostman where he said his abductors weren't Sasquatch but actually a group of First Nations that had lost touch with civilization.

However, the descriptions Ostman gave do not match anything human. As Loxton states, certainly one would be hard pressed to believe a long-lost Indigenous tribe could be eight-feet-tall and covered in hair.

"So, I don't even know how to interpret his claims in terms of basic fact. What was the claim exactly because there seems to be contradictions in it?"

Contradictions like that do fuel the fire of skeptics and generally not ones as intelligent and insightful as Loxton.

The paranormal literature as we know it, and this includes film and television, and our perception of it has been constructed in such a way that it doesn't matter if someone filmed a beaver and said it was Ogopogo. For example, Loxton states that a producer for *Unsolved Mysteries* only cares that whatever was filmed looks a bit mysterious to people living in the city, who have never seen a beaver. The main goal is that people will watch it and get caught up in the narrative.

Loxton and I agree, adding it's important to the people of Kelowna and Tourism Kelowna to have the Ogopogo story to drive tourism to the region. In addition, the tale brings visitors who hope to catch a glimpse of the alleged monster.

Loxton believes it's safe to say the existence of the Loch Ness Monster can be ruled out given the number of search efforts that have been undertaken.

"They've been extreme. They've tried everything. But I'm always going to be a bit in love with that story. It would break my heart if people stopped talking about it."

The same applies to Ogopogo and Lake Okanagan, in my opinion. There have been several expeditions in search of the monster with no concrete evidence to support its existence. It is possible these creatures could leave these bodies of water and go to the ocean, but the journey would be difficult, and one would think there would be more sightings if so. I'd put more weight in the existence of Cadborosaurs given its alleged ability to live in the ocean. With such a massive body of water, the creature therefore has far more room to hunt and hide.

Like Loxton, I don't want these stories to go away or for people to stop believing in the possibility they could exist.

"No that would really hurt me," says Loxton.

The science, however, doesn't add up to something living in these temperate lakes. Loxton says the areas themselves were buried under huge blocks of ice centuries ago. So how would these monsters come to inhabit them in the first place?

"It's hard to get around those things," he admits.

In the end, Loxton believes people who believe they've seen a monster in Lake Okanagan, and other lakes around the world, are seeing a variety of natural things that don't quite add up in their collective minds. To make sense of the sighting they grasp the local folklore. The result is yet another unsubstantiated lake monster sighting.

There are, however, truly interesting sightings like the one we'll investigate firsthand later in this book. That's the picture Colleen Hanson and Dale Hancher took in the fall of 2022. Loxton officially states that he cannot conclude much from the photograph and can't make an educated guess as to what the couple saw.

To venture a guess, he would like to know more about the circumstances surrounding the taking of the picture. He cites the many cases throughout history where the random tourist or witness was an accomplice to the taking of the photograph. This includes legitimate researchers and investigators.

"It can be a lot to untangle. We're stuck with storytelling that is always going to be a bit in doubt and, with this kind of trace evidence, it's always going to be a bit suspicious."

Why would someone perpetuate a hoax, especially someone with an invested interest in proving the existence of a lake monster or Wildman? Having these hoaxes proven as such only hurts the overall case for these monsters possibly being real.

"They want to make cryptozoologists look like idiots," he says. "Sometimes the researchers themselves are pulling the hoaxes so they can present something impressive."

Talking with Loxton is like talking with a kindred spirit. Someone who loves all these stories of monsters and the unknown but who would rather suffer a fact than have faith in a fiction. Through our conversation it felt like I hadn't just met an acquaintance but made a new friend.

By now the clock was beginning to tick down to my own adventure on Lake Okanagan with Eli Watson of Small Town Monsters. Given this would be an expedition of sorts I wanted to talk to someone who had taken part in his own hunt for a lake monster. That turned out to be cryptozoologist Steve Kulls, and I'll detail that conversation next.

To Go in Search of Monsters

The name Steve Kulls should be familiar to those in the cryptozoology community, or anyone with a fascination for Bigfoot and the Loch Ness Monster. A licenced private investigator in the State of New York, he has an extensive background in the gathering, processing, and use of data.

His interest in Bigfoot and related mysteries was sparked as a young boy. Once he hit his teenage years, though, it was replaced by cars and girls and other such pursuits. However, in 1998 Kulls returned to those initial childhood interests by applying his skills as a law-enforcement investigator to the search for Bigfoot. This was something he says started out of a general curiosity about the subject.

"Being an investigator, you get this curiosity of is stuff really real or is it not real? Is it a bunch of B.S. basically?"

His research led to an appearance on History Channel's *MonsterQuest* television series in 2008. The episode, titled *Bigfoot in New York*, was directed by Mike Wafer and Tom Phillips. Wafer liked Kulls' on-camera presence and asked him to lead a team in a Loch Ness Monster documentary he was making for National Geographic.

"Of course I'm not stupid. I was like 'Hell yeah! Let's go!'"

This turned out to be his first stab at researching lake monsters, so he quickly brushed up on Nessie lore. He studied everything from the geology and ecology of the loch to the history of monster sightings in and around it. He was on location for nine days and spent six full days on the water, including a couple of evening expeditions.

"It was a very interesting affair, I have to say," he reminisces.

Having been to Loch Ness on a couple of occasions I can attest to it being an interesting place. Perhaps it's all the stories and folklore, but the region itself has a presence that's hard to ignore.

Did his expedition and investigation at Loch Ness lead Kulls to an opinion on the monster's existence? He said nine days is not enough time to come to any real conclusion on the mystery. On one hand, they had three witnesses take a polygraph test and two passed with flying colors. On the other hand, the one who did not pass was the expedition's boat captain. Several years later, this same captain came forward saying he'd taken close-up pictures of Nessie. Unfortunately, those pictures turned out to be fakes.

"The pictures he produced were actually pictures of the prop used for the recreation during our special. So, I had to call him out on that."

While at Loch Ness, Kulls noticed there was a lot of debris on the water that can be mixed up and confused for a creature in the lake. There were other events too that made him skeptical, including another person claiming to have taken a picture of Nessie.

This person was the greenskeeper at Aldourie Castle. The photo he took was allegedly of Nessie swimming behind said castle, which was where Kulls stayed during the expedition. He says the greenskeeper sold Wafer the rights to use the picture in the documentary, but Kulls expressed doubts about its authenticity.

"It looked too florescent. It was very bright," he mentions of the picture.

Kulls had one day off during the shoot. During that limited break, being an avid cook, he spent some time in the castle's kitchen chatting with the cook while they made lunch together. He asked the cook's opinion of the greenskeeper's photograph and the cook said he didn't think it was real.

The cook believed the photograph showed a reflection of light from across the water, something the cook had seen himself. An hour later Kulls found himself outside and witnessed the same kind of reflection on the loch. He says he was able to recreate the photograph at that time.

In the end, what the greenskeeper claimed was the Loch Ness Monster was actually the sun reflecting off copper flashing on a house across the lake.

"The sun would get to the right angle and hit that and reflect back down onto the loch. So, I took pictures of that. Disappointingly they never put my debunking out there. And they had my photo, but they never used it. And they had some doctor come on at the end and say, 'I think they're a row of boats.' And I'm like 'They're not a row of boats. It's a reflection'."

Kulls expresses that he is all about the truth. Good, bad, or ugly; it doesn't matter. He applies that philosophy to the hunt for evidence of monsters. His experience at Loch Ness creates some doubts about the alleged creature being a long-lost cryptid.

This is all well and good, Hewlett, but what does any of this have to do with Ogopogo? Patience, as I'm getting to that.

Given Kulls led this expedition I wanted to know his methodology when it came to seeking evidence of its existence. I hoped Eli Watson and I could apply a similar methodology during our documentary on Ogopogo.

Kulls and his crew swept the lake with side-scan sonar as they travelled up and down the loch. During night sweeps they used hydrophones, which are used to listen for and record underwater sounds.

Okay, there might not be any money in our budget to trick out a boat with such equipment.

One of the arguments against a large carnivorous creature existing in the lake is a lack of food source, but the hydrophones Kulls used were able to pick up a large school of salmon living beneath the surface.

"As you're going up and down the loch there's a lot of fishermen there," explains Kulls. "So, if there's no source of food, then why is there all of these salmon fishermen there?"

There's also a large salmon population in Lake Okanagan, supporting the theory that a similar large carnivorous creature could exist there, as Ken Gerhard pointed out earlier. In fact, as Gerhard pointed out, Lake Okanagan and Loch Ness are similar in a variety of ways. Check back to the first chapter in this book to refresh your memory.

What sets Loch Ness apart from other glacial-carved lakes, as far as Kulls is concerned, is the fact it's surrounded by peat moss which creates very poor visibility in the water. He said the expedition put divers in the lake at Urguhart Castle and they couldn't see much beyond three feet in front of them. This would make it easier for a large creature to swim about undetected by the naked eye.

"You could scoop up the water, and it looks muddy," he describes.

So, if money was no object, what would Kulls suggest we do during our expedition to increase our chances of finding evidence of Ogopogo? Kulls admits he's not as familiar with Ogopogo and Lake Okanagan as he is Loch Ness and Nessie, but he has a few ideas.

His first bit of advice is to be methodical and find out where any pertinent ecological or geographical structures like underwater caves or canyons are.

"Think about where a creature would go to remain hidden or remain undisturbed," he expounds, adding most aquatic life prefers to be left alone.

"So that's where I would kind of focus my search rings on."

If possible, have good sonar equipment on board the vessel and be diligent in working out search patterns in an organized pattern, he adds. Hydrophones could be used as well but it can be hard to determine what any sound it picks up is created by, especially if we have no baseline to go from. What does Ogopogo sound like? No one is sure.

Rattlesnake Island to the south of Kelowna is believed by many to be home to Ogopogo, both by the local Indigenous population and tourism officials. This is largely due to a series of underwater caves beneath the island itself. So, we've got a starting point for any search we do.

When it comes to witness accounts and stories passed down about creatures like Ogopogo, Kulls believes they have value to any investigator or researcher. He gets into debates with skeptics and our colleagues within the cryptozoology community alike when it comes to what people call anecdotal evidence.

"They will say 'You know all we have is anecdotal evidence.' Well, what is anecdotal evidence? 'Somebody sees a Bigfoot or somebody sees a Loch Ness Monster and that's anecdotal.' No, it's not. That's actually direct testimony," said Kulls.

"Anecdotal evidence is you hear something that you can't identify and you say, 'I heard this unidentified stuff and there's sightings in this area so that's probably what it is.' That's anecdotal evidence."

Me explaining to Kulls there are stories about a lake monster associated with Rattlesnake Island is anecdotal evidence, he explains. If somebody says they saw Ogopogo swimming by Rattlesnake Island, that's not anecdotal. That's direct testimony.

He takes issue with skeptics who claim witnesses provide the worst kind of evidence. In police work, much of the prosecution's case is based on witness testimony. Yes, accounts of the same crime – say a man with gun in hand running out of a store that's just been robbed – may differ, but it's up to the investigator to piece together the common variables these witnesses provide and put forward a case for the courts.

"How is that (information) not reliable?" he said, adding the same applies to cryptid research.

I took this as a good sign that any witnesses to Ogopogo sightings we find are worth our time.

As we go deeper into this volume, you'll see how much Western culture has misappropriated First Nations' beliefs and spirituality and made it our own. The name Ogopogo isn't even the creature's true identity! For Indigenous people, these monsters aren't monsters at all, but spirits important to their culture. This begs the question: what does Kulls make of the possible paranormal origins of beings like Nessie and Ogopogo? Does he put any stock or thought into them not being flesh-and-blood animals?

To answer, Kulls took the discussion back to Sasquatch, saying he's seen an adult and a juvenile on separate occasions. In both cases there was track evidence left behind. As far as he's concerned, that makes these animals real beings.

"It disappeared but not that it dematerialized. It disappeared like a deer would. Into the forest and gone."

A lot of Native American/First Nations accounts attribute many animals as being supernatural beings: eagles, falcons, coyotes, and wolves to name just a few, explains Kulls. The same is true in other cultures around the world. They were given supernatural attributes at a time when these animals were then largely unknown to humans and required explanation.

"Dolphins were thought to be mermaids. Manatees were thought to be mermaids. So, there's a lot of anthropomorphism. The ability for us to relay human characteristics or god-like characteristics to animals," Kulls explains.

"Do I believe they (Bigfoot, Nessie and Ogopogo) are supernatural? No."

Even Native American stories of Sasquatch kidnapping human women and children are more urban legend than anything else. He said such stories were made up to scare women and children into not venturing into the woods alone.

That's not to say Kulls doesn't keep an open mind when it comes to studying and searching for cryptids like Nessie and Bigfoot, but he believes it's important to work within the laws of science and nature, not folklore.

Whatever your findings, always tell the truth whether you find something or not. This is done on a case-by-case basis. Just because you find some kind of evidence supporting the existence of a lake monster on one quest doesn't mean every future investigation will produce the same results, he reminds me.

"You look at the cases separately and, if you find a common thread, you might have something."

This means it's important to keep your emotions in check, something people in the paranormal field have a hard time doing, he asserts. I agree and believe these emotions cloud one's judgment when it comes to accepting and denying potential evidence. It's good to be passionate about the subject, but each investigation needs to be approached with reason, logic, and emotional detachment, almost like being an outsider on the subject.

So, then, what does Kulls think Nessie, Ogopogo and other lake monsters are? Given the body of evidence collected so far, these creatures could be anything from a yet undiscovered species to a misidentified known animal or phenomenon. But, given the limited geography of a lake, he can't say for certain there's some strange creature living in these bodies of water.

"I'm not poo-pooing it. I'm definitely not shooting down what people have seen. I'm just going with the odds here. But it definitely warrants to be investigated, and it should be investigated vigorously and without any type of bias."

Perhaps it's our shared investigative background, but it feels like Kulls and I are not only on the same page when it comes to the possible existence of lake monsters, but also in how one should investigate not only this phenomenon, but all high strangeness.

With the bulk of my research complete it was time to pack my bags and head to Kelowna to join Eli Watson for our own investigation into the lake monster known as Ogopogo!

And the Adventure Begins

It's not every day you get invited to film a documentary on Ogopogo, but that's exactly what happened to me in January of 2023.

I'd first "met" Eli Watson in the summer of 2020. I say "met" because we didn't actually meet in person until I joined him in Kelowna, British Columbia to film the Ogopogo documentary for Small Town Monsters. Eli was one of the first people to interview me after the launch of our web series *We Want to Believe* as part of a promotional tour for the show, which ran on *JoBlo Horror Videos* at the time.

Eli is a co-host of the popular monster-themed podcast *Cryptid Campfire* alongside Jasmine With and Alexander Daikaiju. With and Daikaiju weren't present for the interview, so it was just Eli and I talking ghosts and Sasquatch for about an hour, and we really hit it off. Eli has a relaxed, easygoing manner and the conversation flowed easily. We kept in touch via social media, which doesn't often happen between interviewer and interviewee, and even ended up working together when *Cryptid Campfire* became a video podcast on the *Paranormal Network* YouTube channel that I managed for *JoBlo*.

The show, and my time with the YouTube channel, eventually parted ways but Eli and I continued to stay in touch. He went to work for Seth Breedlove at Small Town

Monsters, and I entered the land of freelance writing and content creation.

It's while interviewing Eli for an article for *Paranormality Magazine* that he informed me Small Town Monsters was venturing to Harrison Hot Springs here in British Columbia to film a documentary on the origins of Sasquatch, and he would spend part of the time in Kelowna making the Ogopogo documentary.

"How far away are you from Kelowna?" Eli asked.

"Kamloops is like two hours away," I said. "Why?"

"Did you want to join me? I could interview you…"

"When are you guys going to be here?"

The plan was for Small Town Monsters to set down sometime in May. I agreed on the spot to join Eli, only mentioning it to my long-suffering wife after the fact (always better to ask forgiveness than permission). And before the interview was over, I'd agreed to not only be interviewed for Eli's documentary but would join him for the duration of the shoot.

Suffice to say, I was excited.

Growing up in Kamloops, British Columbia one of my family's favorite vacation spots was Kelowna, a city of similar size in population but with better malls for shopping – which appealed to my mom – and a more picturesque setting given it bordered Lake Okanagan. It was close; getting there was an easy two-hour drive as opposed to the four hours it took to get to the large city of Vancouver.

My father and I enjoyed spending a couple of nights in a hotel with a pool and the chance to eat out, which we rarely did while at home. My young self also liked the idea of spending time in a town with a monster.

The first time I saw Ogopogo was in the form of a public art statue that resides along the Kelowna waterfront. The statue, which depicts a friendly looking serpent with a horse-like head, is made of painted fibreglass and was built in 1960 by Peter Soelin. Every time our family stayed in Kelowna, I would ask to visit the statue. The idea that such a creature could exist in a lake so close to where I lived fascinated me.

It didn't take long to notice the friendly lake monster's likeness on postcards, hats and even T-shirts. As I grew up, it became clear the city of Kelowna had adopted Ogopogo as a tourist draw.

Indeed, if you go to the Tourism Kelowna website today there's a whole section dedicated to the legend of Ogopogo, stating stories go back thousands of years to when the Interior Salish First Nations discussed the spirit of the lake, *N'ha-a-itk*. European settlers transformed those stories into the Ogopogo as sightings continued.

As I grew older, I realized many people who visited Lake Okanagan, or had lived on or near it, had a lake monster story. Even my Uncle David believes he saw something out on the lake he couldn't explain, and he doesn't believe in such things.

To help film a documentary on Ogopogo, talk to witnesses and researchers about it, and potentially venture out on the lake itself in search of answers was too good an opportunity to pass up.

I was also excited to meet Eli in person. We had become friends through our online connections and collaborations, and to be able to cement that friendship face to face was also a rare opportunity.

The offer also came at almost the exact same time I decided to write this book. I'd already begun researching the subject and reaching out to potential interviewees. Not believing in coincidences, this book and the accompanying documentary were meant to be.

So, we agreed to keep in touch through the ensuing months. Eli would put together travel plans and connect with people he wanted to include in the documentary, and I'd do the same for the book. We agreed elements of this book and his show could be included in each other's finished product. In the end, both would be a collaborative effort.

I spent months researching Ogopogo and making notes. It's during this time that I connected with Daniel Loxton and Steve Kulls, whose thoughts on the subject you've already read, and picked the brains of friends and colleagues Peter Renn and Kenney W. Irish. I also had an unpleasant exchange with a University of British Columbia professor who had been featured in a television news story about Ogopogo but refused to share his thoughts in this book.

Here's a bit of what I picked up during my research.

The first reported encounter with non-Indigenous people occurred in 1855 when Metis settler John McDougall was crossing the lake with his horses tied behind his canoe, which he'd done several times before. The horses were pulled under the water by some mysterious force and McDougall was forced to cut the ropes attaching the animals to his canoe for fear of being hauled under himself.

Ogopogo wasn't witnessed by a European settler until 1872 when Susan Allison claimed she'd seen what she described as a dinosaur in the lake.

Digging into the legend further, one finds some spectacular details, such as the Salish people would sacrifice animals to *N'ha-a-itk* before travelling on the lake near the monster's home at Rattlesnake Island to guarantee safe passage. Reading that, and the ferocious story of McDougall's horses, leads one to believe Ogopogo is a fierce creature and nothing like the one depicted by Soelin's friendly statue.

As with any such story, it can be hard to separate fact from fantasy. Yes, even stories about monsters can have an element of truth in them. But when such stories are adopted for tourism's sake such details can become even more muddied. Let's face it, when it comes to turning these stories into entertainment, even the most mundane details can be turned into something wild and scary. Just look at the number of movies based on alleged true ghost stories.

Case in point, the 2016 horror film *The Conjuring 2*, which is the second movie based on the case files of Ed and Lorraine Warren, two pioneers in the field of paranormal investigations. The movie is about the Enfield Poltergeist case that rocked England during the 1970s, and plants the Warrens smack dab in the middle of it. Whether or not you believe the story of the Enfield poltergeist, if you do any research, you'll quickly discover the Warrens had nothing to do with the investigation. In fact, they weren't allowed anywhere near 284 Green Street nor the Hodgson family who claimed to experience this activity. Yet, the movie begins with the title card *Based on the True Story*.

The problem is people tend to believe these highly fictional accounts as gospel truth and that fuels a popular misconception about the actual stories behind them. This is especially true when it comes to the paranormal.

I had reached out to Tourism Kelowna to get their thoughts on Ogopogo and was quickly redirected to the Westbank First Nation. I had to wonder if Tourism Kelowna's unwillingness to talk about their beloved mascot had something to do with a 2021 move by the nearby city of Vernon that gave the Ogopogo copyright back to Sylix Nation, which is the Indigenous people of the Okanagan.

Yes, the name Ogopogo was actually owned by a municipality! The intellectual property was given to the city of Vernon in 1956 from previous copyright holder A.G. Seabrook. In fact, Ogopogo is a made-up word and has no relation to Indigenous beliefs about *N'ha-a-itk*.

So, I reached out to the Westbank First Nation and requested an interview. I was delighted when they agreed. You'll read the interview with Coralee Miller, the Museum Docent for the Sncewips Heritage Museum in Kelowna, and a member of the Westbank First Nation, later in Eli and I's adventures.

It must be stated here, though, that for Miller and her people, Ogopogo is far more than a folk story and tourist attraction. It's an integral part of their culture and belief system. In fact, the name Ogopogo was created by 1920 folk singers and came from the song *The Funny Foxtrot*, which was sung in the Vernon dance halls of the day, so we can see why the municipality of Vernon was interested in laying claim to the name.

I find this little detour fascinating. Harkening back to my point earlier about the existence of lake monsters being impossible, the concept becomes more possible under the Indigenous belief system. If Ogopogo isn't a flesh-and-blood creature but rather a water spirit that is the very embodiment of the lake itself, then all the earthly arguments against its existence are thrown out the window. Ditto the limited number of sightings when, as Miller will point out, you only see *N'ha-a-itk* when *N'ha-a-itk* wants to be seen.

This point of view is turning up in the Bigfoot community as well, with more and more researchers taking the concept of "paranormal Bigfoot" seriously. In fact, there's a big debate between the flesh-and-blood camp and the paranormal camp in this regard, with believers on the paranormal side of the fence accusing the flesh-and-blood researchers of omitting paranormal elements from experiencer reports.

I've never liked explaining an unknown with another unknown, but Indigenous beliefs – which date back long before settlers landed on these shores – can't be ignored either. Increasingly I'm finding myself in the camp that believes these "monsters" aren't as tangible as we'd like them to be. The time Eli and I spent together on this documentary cemented this idea further.

Obviously, more on that later.

What surprised me was how few people were willing to talk about Ogopogo with me. Only Collen Hanson and Dale Hanchar, who took the picture that surfaced in October 2022, agreed to be interviewed for the book and subsequent documentary. Another witness who turned up on the television news said he wasn't interested in talking about his sighting and the footage he shot… unless we were willing to pay him.

We weren't.

Eli was able to connect with Laurie Gaal, daughter of famed Ogopogo researcher and author Arlene Gaal, who was mentioned earlier in this book. Gaal inherited all her mother's research material, plus all manner of Ogopogo films and data she'd gathered during her years of research. Eli was most interested in getting permission to use the famed Folden Film for the documentary, and we hoped to connect with Laurie during our time in Kelowna about that.

The Folden footage was shot by Art Folden in August of 1968 and it's the first time anyone captured what could be the elusive lake monster on film. Folden and his wife were driving along Highway 97 when they noticed something strange in the water. The couple pulled off the road and Folden grabbed his 8mm camera, wanting to get a picture of what he estimated to be a forty-foot mass moving in the lake.

As Folden later explained, he filmed the long, serpentine-like form as it moved across the surface and stopped filming whenever it dove underwater. Folden estimated the object was about three hundred yards offshore and was moving from shallow to deeper water.

Ogopogo enthusiasts believe this to be a compelling piece of evidence, while skeptics believe Folden filmed nothing more than a log moving fast along the surface of the lake. Others believe he might have filmed two creatures on the lake, swimming close together.

Interestingly, Larry Thal filmed a similar creature with his home-movie camera twelve years later. Thal was filming his wife and kids when, according to him, something strange appeared – a large, dark appendage that moved out of the water.

According to Thal, whatever he filmed swam about for forty-five minutes in front of some fifty tourists and his family. Unfortunately, the footage itself is only about ten seconds long.

Arlene Gaal has commented that the creature Folden filmed, and the one capture on camera by Thal, are basically the same size. She is quoted as saying Thal's film also provides a good idea of how fast the animal swims and the massive waves it creates.

Another person Eli and I sought out was Bill Steciuk. A Kelowna-based retiree, Steciuk is also one of the leading Ogopogo researchers. He runs a website called *Ogopogo Quest*, which includes a detailed history of the creature and a database of sightings ranging from historical to recent, as well as a means for witnesses to submit their own.

Combing through Steciuk's website, it's clear one could lose themselves for hours going over the material the man has amassed. It's no wonder he's earned the nickname Legend Hunter and has been featured in so many news stories about Ogopogo and on episodes of *MonsterQuest* and *America's Monsters*.

I'd reached out to him prior to Eli inviting me to the shoot. Steciuk replied to my email, saying he'd be interested in talking to me but that he was recovering from an illness and would be out of commission for a while. I followed up with him a month or so later, but he never responded to my email. I passed his name on to Eli, who said he'd follow up with him.

Months went by with Eli and I keeping in close contact as elements of the expedition came together. Hanchar and Hanson agreed to meet with us and even take us out in their sailboat to where they had their sighting. Miller also agreed to meet with us at the museum and arrange a trip out to Ogopogo's alleged lair at Rattlesnake Island. Eli was even able to get in contact with Steciuk, who agreed to an interview and expressed an interest in meeting Hanchar and Hanson as well. Eli also set up an interview with Andrew McKay, who ran the *Into the Portal* podcast. McKay had talked Ogopogo on an episode of *Cryptid Campfire* and Eli believed he could provide some great information for the documentary.

In mid-April Eli confirmed dates for his trip, which ended up being May 11 to 17, giving us a few weeks to nail down any final details. This included how he'd get from Vancouver International Airport to Kelowna as the rest of the Small Town Monsters crew would be staying in the city of Chilliwack, a good couple of hours drive away. I offered to pick Eli up in Chilliwack, get him to Kelowna, then back to Chilliwack as he'd become part of the crew for their upcoming Bigfoot documentary, *On the Trail of Bigfoot: The Origin*.

What we didn't have was a boat to take us to Rattlesnake Island. Westbank First Nations couldn't provide one and Hanchar and Hanson said it would take them a good five or more hours to sail us there and back, which we just couldn't afford timewise. We had less than seventy-two hours to film a feature-length documentary and would be moving a mile a minute the entire time.

Fortunately, Bill Steciuk came to the rescue. He was able to charter us a boat at a special rate and agreed to pilot it for us as well. This proved a big win for the documentary as we'd not only interview Steciuk, but we could do so during an excursion to Rattlesnake Island. Miller would also join us on the expedition to provide insight into her people's practices when venturing into *N'ha-a-itk*'s realm. This would become a highlight of the trip.

Then, less than forty-hours before Eli was scheduled to touchdown in British Columbia and filming was to start, everything almost fell apart.

Seth Breedlove's mother passed away after a lengthy cancer battle, and it looked like he wouldn't be able to make the journey to Canada and direct the Bigfoot documentary. This would mean Eli might have to step in for him, which meant the Ogopogo project wouldn't happen at all. This would have been unfortunate, but understandable given the circumstances. Fortunately, the decision was made that the crew could begin filming *On the Trail of Bigfoot: The Origin* with Eli providing direction from Kelowna.

Why not cancel both productions given the circumstances, you might ask? Documentaries like these take months, even a year to plan, especially one with the scope of *On the Trail of Bigfoot*. It can be a logistical nightmare which, in this case, involved people in the United States and Canada. The show literally had to go on.

Eli and I met virtually several times a day leading up to his arrival and he phoned me the day before I was scheduled to meet him saying some of the film crew's flight had been delayed, meaning he'd land on the morning of May 11 and not have a means of getting to Chilliwack, where I was scheduled to meet him. The drive was several hours out of the way for me, and Eli decided he'd rather rent a car and drive to Kelowna, where I'd pick him up and head for our hotel and first night of filming.

Writing all this now in hindsight, none of it seems like a big deal. But at the time it made for a stressful couple of days.

One of the big concerns on Eli's and my mind at the time was how we'd get along and work together. Sure, we'd interacted online, but we'd never spent any time together in person. How we gelled as people could make or break this experience and impact the finished film.

The big day arrived without much fanfare. I packed up a suitcase full of clothes, my trusty adventuring hat, and camera and audio-recording equipment, spent some extra time with my wife and son, and hit the road on the afternoon of May 11. Eli had touched down that morning and had about a four-hour drive to Kelowna. I tried to time my arrival so that I didn't have too long of a wait. In the end, I spent about an hour at a Starbucks before he pulled into the car rental outlet at Kelowna International Airport, and I drove up to meet him.

Eli was visibly tired as he tossed his luggage into the back of my truck. We had time for a quick handshake before he got into the passenger's seat and we pulled out of the busy lot, a long line of vehicles and tired passengers behind us.

We got the small talk out of the way. You know, "How was your flight?" and "How was the drive?" kind of stuff. He'd had a heck of a time getting through customs and the officers literally took everything out of his pack.

"What happened?" I asked.

"They asked me why I was in Canada," Eli said. "And I told them 'Looking for Ogopogo' and they rolled their heads and were like 'Oh, what is this Ogopogo you speak of?'."

They asked Eli to step aside and open his bags, pulling out his camera equipment and several books on everything from UFOs to Bigfoot and, of course, Ogopogo.

"You're pretty serious about this stuff," one of the guards said to him.

"Yeah. This is my job," Eli told them.

The situation improved from there and Eli was soon on his way... after he repacked everything.

Despite him being tired, it didn't take long for Eli and I to find a friendly rhythm to our conversation. We found our hotel and checked in. He wanted some time to get settled after a long day of travelling and I wanted to pick up some drinks to enjoy after our days of filming. We agreed to take an hour or so to unwind before we contemplated dinner and ironing out any last-minute details.

To pass the time I went for a walk, finding a cold beer and wine store and taking in some of the sights. As I said earlier, I'd been coming to Kelowna since I was a child and the city, like me, had grown and changed a lot. Any small city vibe had long since been replaced with modern high rises that dwarfed the original buildings, each new structure stretching higher into the sky then the last. The flow of traffic that passed west and east, and east to west, along Highway 97 had grown to big city levels of congestion. Unlike my hometown of Kamloops, Kelowna grew fast once people discovered its pristine scenery and wineries, which were plentiful due to the warm climate, making it a perfect region for growing grapes and other fruit.

Of course, there is Lake Okanagan itself, which the city of Kelowna has capitalized on by developing a large park and marina along it near the city centre. Suffice to say, the lake is one of Kelowna's main attractions.

The lake…and the monster said to dwell within it.

Kelowna started as a settlement some twelve thousand years ago in what is now called the Okanagan Valley. The Sylix people were the first to live there, thriving on hunting, fishing, gathering, and trading with other tribes and the first European settlement, which was formed in 1859 by three Oblate missionaries, Father Pandosy, Father Richard, and Brother Surel. Some of this original settlement remains today at the Father Pandosy Mission Provincial Site.

In 1893, Canada's Governor General at the time, Lord Aberdeen, bought huge tracts of land in the valley as a means of recognizing the region's fruit growing potential, setting the stage for the orchards and wineries to come.

The name Kelowna comes from the story of August Gillard, an early settler who is said to have crawled from an underground shelter just as some Sylix people passed by. One of them called out *"Kim-ach-touch"* when they saw him, a phrase meaning brown bear. Over time, *"Kim-ach-touch"* became Kelowna, which means grizzly bear and is easier to pronounce.

When Kelowna became a city in 1905, it had a population of just six hundred people. It is now home to more than two hundred and twenty thousand, a number that swells with tourists during the hot summer months.

Many of these tourists come to enjoy the scenery, the wines, boating, and sailing. But others, like Eli and I, come to scour the waters in hope of seeing Ogopogo. Tourism Kelowna knows this, which is why Ogopogo – or Ogie as the creature is affectionately known – adorns everything from postcards to T-shirts to hats and even stuffed animals.

All this flowed through my mind as I walked back to the hotel with some cold drinks in hand. Then I received a text from Eli saying he was rested and ready to meet up. I told him I was a few minutes out and hurried back to the hotel. It would seem our adventure was officially ready to get underway.

Not Just a Children's Story

"Seth's coming," Eli told me as I opened the door to my hotel room.

I'd rushed back to the hotel and had just placed my drinks in a fridge when Eli knocked on my door. He'd spoken with a member of the Small Town Monsters team and learned Breedlove had decided to fly out the next day and take the helm of the Bigfoot documentary. This took the pressure off Eli to try to direct the film from a distance while also spearheading his Ogopogo filming. He'd have one phone meeting with the crew in Chilliwack the following morning and that would be it.

"That's good news, man," I said, stepping out into the warm sun and closing the door behind me.

"Yeah, this will make things a lot easier."

Our plan for night one was simple: food and shooting some B-roll, which is essentially footage of the lake and surrounding scenery; anything that can be used to bridge scenes or transition one shot to another. B-roll is often used as "floating" imagery during a narration as well. Once we decided on where to eat, we'd head to Kelowna City Park to catch some sunset shots of the lake and Peter Soelin's infamous Ogopogo statue.

But first, we needed to eat!

Eli was up for Chinese food, as was I. We asked the hotel clerk to recommend a Chinese food restaurant, and she gave us several options, the closest being just down the block, so we ventured there first.

I pulled my Dodge into the heavy rush-hour traffic, and Eli and I got to talking. He'd never been to Canada before and was already marveling at the mountains, which he said rivalled those in Alaska, and the beauty of the Okanagan Valley. He was also excited to be working with me, and I with him.

Minutes later we arrived at the Chinese food restaurant, which was open but only for take out, so we headed to the second option our clerk had recommended.

It was closed.

I punched Chinese restaurants into my Google Maps and found another one nearby with a good rating and we drove there. It was closing in five minutes.

This went on for some time before we found a restaurant that was open, had a decent rating, and wouldn't close before we could finish eating. The meal was well worth the effort to find it, and Eli and I enjoyed some good getting-to-know-you banter about two of our favorite things: movies and the paranormal.

As with many of us in this field, Eli's interest in mysteries and monsters was sparked as a young boy when his dad introduced him to the History Channel docuseries *MonsterQuest*. *MonsterQuest* produced sixty-eight episodes during its four seasons and took a scientific approach in its quest to prove or disprove the existence of creatures like

Bigfoot and the Loch Ness Monster. There was even an episode on Ogopogo featuring Steciuk!

Eli knew then that looking for these creatures wasn't a normal pursuit – not that he likes using the term normal – but the prospect of doing so thrilled him. When he met other like-minded people working at a movie theatre, Daikaiju and With, their conversations sparked the idea of creating a cryptozoology-themed podcast. It was With who coined the title *Cryptid Campfire*.

Cryptid Campfire episodes offer a deep dive into a variety of cryptids both well-known and little known, like the Owlman of Mawnan Smith and the Ningen, as well as featured interviews with various researchers and experiencers. As the podcast's popularity grew, people began reaching out to the trio via *Cryptid Campfire*'s social media and website. This included producers wanting them to appear on TV shows and documentaries.

It was an interview with Alexsandar Petakov and Nash Hoover that set Eli on his current path as a documentary filmmaker. Hoover and Petakov were part of a program called *Chasing Legends*, which follows a pair of cousins who travel the globe investigating various alleged monsters. Eli met the duo face to face, they hit off, and he ended up doing a lot of postproduction work on the series.

By the time his work on *Chasing Legends* debuted in 2021, Petakov had been working with Breedlove on Small Town Monsters productions. Eli asked Petakov to help him land an interview with Breedlove on *Cryptid Campfire*, and the two ended up talking monsters after Breedlove's official interview was over.

"We talked for like more than an hour," he told me, still surprised by that initial connection.

During that conversation Breedlove presented Watson with the opportunity to join a Small Town Monsters production. The rest is, as the cliché goes, history.

We wrapped up our meal, paid the bill, and drove to the park. The nice thing about a city the size of Kelowna is that it doesn't take long to get anywhere, and we pulled into a spot just minutes after eating.

The park was busy! It was a Thursday night in the spring, but it might as well have been a summer holiday weekend. People rollerbladed by us or rode bikes. Couples walked hand in hand. Groups of youth sprawled out on blankets and laughed. Street musicians performed with varying degrees of talent. After two years of avoiding each other, people were happy to gather again.

We carefully navigated our way to the beach, doing our best to stay out of anyone's path. Eli pulled out his Sony video camera and began shooting footage of the setting sun, which sparkled across the water and bounced off boats as they passed.

My role at this point was to observe. Observe and find the Ogopogo statue.

Every time our family visited Kelowna when I was a boy, I insisted my parents take me to see Soelin's statue. It was just this thing I had to do. I even insisted on taking my son to see it when we visited Kelowna to attend my sister-in-law's graduation ceremony. Given the number of times that I'd stood beside the statue you'd think I'd know where it was off the top of my head.

You'd think wrong.

Eli and I wandered around the park for a good fifteen or twenty minutes before I finally gave up and used Google Maps to lead us to it. It's funny how one's memories deceive us, as I always believed the statue was further into the park when, in fact, it sits right near the park's entrance at Bernard Avenue.

What had confused me, we later learned, was there used to be two Ogopogo statues in the park. The one Soelin was commissioned to build and another of Ogopogo's head that children could climb on using a series of ropes. I even got a picture of my son atop this statue back in 2018, but it's since been removed by the City of Kelowna due to public-safety concerns.

Author's son, Griffon, atop the now defunct Ogopogo statue in Kelowna

For the record, there's also a third statue of Ogopogo that rests thirty feet below the surface of Lake Okanagan at Paul's Tomb, just left of the bay in Knox Mountain Park. This statue is about eight-feet-tall and fourteen-feet-long and would make a great destination for any SCUBA diver who wouldn't panic at the sight of it.

Eli and I eventually navigated our way to Soelin's friendly depiction of Lake Okanagan's famous resident, and Eli started filming from several different angles, patiently waiting for a family of cyclists to move on so they wouldn't be in the shot. He also took a picture of the statue's face, intending to do a comparison with the photograph Hanchar and Hanson took in October of 2022.

Curious, we brought up the Hanchar/Hanson photo and held it beside the head of the Soelin statue. What we found most interesting is the head as depicted on the statue was eerily similar to the picture Hanchar and Hanson took.

The face has a similar shape, with a long snout with eyes set on either side of it. There're the two nodules poking up out of the water in the photo, which are also depicted on the statue. The only difference is the statue has a friendly disposition while whatever is in the photograph looks very much alive and not the work of a children' story.

"It looks pretty much the same, dude," Eli said to me. "Wonder if they actually shot Ogopogo?"

This is a question we'd ask ourselves more and more frequently during the next few days.

We continued filming B roll, wandering onto the marina dock as the sun set behind the mountains. Eli marvelled at the beauty of the Okanagan, a sight I'd long since started taking for granted. His comments made me pause – I really did live in a beautiful part of the world.

My thoughts went back to that family trip to my sister-in-law's graduation in 2018. My son was six at the time and sitting through a long graduation ceremony just wasn't in the cards, so he and I excused ourselves and wandered down to this very park. I showed him the Soelin statue then took him to the one he could climb on. He scampered and struggled his way to the top. Once back on solid ground, he asked several questions about Ogopogo; what it was, where it lived, and was it friendly?

I shared with him the theories, which I covered in the earlier conversation with Gerhard, and said Ogopogo was supposed to live in caves near Rattlesnake Island. As for it being friendly, I omitted anything I'd heard to the contrary at that point.

"Did the Ogopogo statue look scary?" I asked him, practicing something my father always did-answering a difficult question with a question.

"No," my boy replied. "He looked nice."

"There you go. He's a friendly monster."

Griffon seemed satisfied with this, and ran onto a nearby dock, making a beeline for the end, which stretched several meters out onto the lake. As he neared the edge, he slowed, his footsteps becoming cautious. He craned first his torso and then his neck out over the end of the dock, peering into the water, but being careful not to get too close.

I laughed. "What are you doing, son?"

"Looking for Ogopogo, dad. But I don't want him to get me."

I guessed that even when something appears friendly it's still best to err on the side of caution. That thought made me a little sad.

Griffon cautiously searching for Ogopogo

Snapping back to the present, Eli was now on the phone with the Small Town Monsters team, who had just arrived at their accommodations in Chilliwack. I checked the time and decided I should give Griffon a call and wish him good night. His bedtime was fast approaching.

We talked a bit about his day and mine, and we agreed we'd each had a good day. I was wishing him good night and telling him I loved him when he asked when I'd be home?

"I'll be back before you get home from school on Monday, bud."

"Good. I can't wait. I miss you."

"I miss you too, pal."

We said our love you's and I clicked off. I lived for experiences like this but missed my son deeply. He was growing up fast and such excursions meant I missed his first steps and other milestones. I was beginning to wonder if it was all worth it.

"Everything good?" Eli broke my melancholic train of thought.

"Yup. All good. You?"

Eli nodded. "Got what I need. We should pick up some cigars and head back to the hotel."

I agreed that would be a good idea and we ventured back to the truck. Eli was an avid pipe smoker, and I enjoy a good cigar now and then. So, we found a smoke shop that was still open, and I picked up a couple of cigars for what would become a nightly ritual during this adventure: Eli puffing on his pipe, me chomping down on a stogie, and us engaging in several in-depth discussions about everything from politics to the paranormal.

I don't know about you, but I've never slept well in hotel rooms. It might have been the anticipation of really getting rolling the next morning or just being in a new, noisy environment, but I slept lightly that first night in Kelowna.

Eli, who had been up for about twenty-four hours, slept like the dead.

The next morning, I awoke, and, after a quick cup of hotel-room coffee and a shower, I phoned my Canadian Paranormal Society colleague and friend Olivier Asselin. Eli was in need of someone to shoot drone footage as Canada's drone operating laws are different than those in the United States. Rather than risk flying his drone during the shoot, and possibly getting caught and fined for it, Eli asked if I knew anyone with a drone. Olivier has shot drone footage for our *We Want to Believe* documentary series and, when I approached him about it, he jumped at the chance to not only go looking for Ogopogo but film some footage for this Small Town Monsters production.

I caught Asselin on the way to work and arranged to have him meet Eli and I the next morning at Hotel Eldorado, a resort located along the eastern bank of Lake Okanagan which has a marina attached. This was also where we were scheduled to join Bill Steciuk for our expedition to Rattlesnake Island.

"I'm so stoked man. I can't wait," Asselin said with his trademark enthusiasm.

He's younger than me by a good twenty years but has an unnatural maturity for a man his age, something he picked up during a few rough years on the streets. But that maturity never dampened his energy and excitement for life.

We met in late 2021 when he attended a presentation I and my friend and Canadian Paranormal Society co-founder, Peter Renn, hosted at a historic ranch with a long history of paranormal activity. We were introduced after the presentation and accompanying ghost tours and got to talking. Asselin is an inventor and has crafted his own ghost hunting equipment, everything from motion detectors to trigger objects, and he was keen to learn more about the field. Peter and I ended up inviting him on an investigation a month later and he quickly became a valuable member of our team.

The next day's arrangements made, I texted Eli and we soon met outside our hotel. After a quick pancake breakfast, we ventured out to meet Hanson and Hanchar. The plan was to meet them at their home but when I called the couple to let them know we were on our way, they asked us to meet them at the Hotel Eldorado! Yes, the same Hotel Eldorado we were headed to the following morning.

"That's where we put our boat in the water," said Hanchar. "Figured we'd save some time and just meet you guys there if you're okay with doing the interview on the water?"

Naturally, we were. So off to Hotel Eldorado we went.

Our first challenge was finding a parking spot. The weather was perfect; sunny without a cloud in the sky and temperatures that would climb into the mid-thirties in Canadian Celsius, or well into the seventies for our American readers. It was the first day of a prolonged, and unseasonably hot, heatwave and that meant people were heading to the lake in droves.

Pulling into the lot, every stall was full and there was no room to accommodate my pickup truck. It was a Friday, and I thought more people would be at work, but the weather obviously convinced many to take an extra day off. This was the first decent day we'd had all year, and I didn't bemoan anyone who wanted to take advantage of it.

We ended up parking in a small lot at a nearby park and unpacked what gear we needed for our excursion on Hanchar and Hanson's sailboat.

"What do you want me to do?" I asked Eli.

"If you can use the GoPro that would be great," said Eli. "Shoot everything and anything. Whatever you can."

"You got it, brother."

I slung my satchel pack over my shoulder and powered up one of my two GoPros while Eli put his backpack over his shoulder and held his Sony camcorder at the ready. We made our way to the Eldorado, passing a construction site on the way. One of the workers complimented Eli on his trademark cowboy hat and goatee, which I think left him a little startled.

It didn't take long to spot Hanchar and Hanson. I'd already interviewed them once for this book via Zoom, so I knew what they looked like. But the white and ocean green sailboat – a good twenty-five-to-thirty-footer – stood out right away and we quickly made out Hanchar, Hanson and their friend, Myrna Germaine, as they readied the vessel for sailing.

"Hello Jason!" Hanson said to me in greeting. She'd remembered me from our Zoom chat as well. I reached out my hand and shook hers, saying hello back, and introduced Eli. A quick round of introductions was made, and Eli and I offered to help ready the boat. Hanchar told us it was almost ready to go, so I filmed the process while Eli spoke with Hanson and Germaine who, it turned out, was with the couple on the day they took their photograph.

Hanchar hopped in his truck and began backing the sailboat down a ramp to the lake while Hanson and Germaine guided him. I filmed Eli walking to the dock as boat and trailer slid into the water alongside it.

"Have either of you sailed before?" Hanson wanted to know.

Eli had but I hadn't, although I'd been out in boats before. She followed up by asking how comfortable we were out on the water. Having grown up on a lake, being on or in the water was second nature to me.

"I know how to swim," Eli said to the camera. "Plus, with all the weight I've gained, I'll probably float on my own."

We laughed. "Well, after that IHOP breakfast yah," I said to keep the joke going.

Several minutes passed before Hanchar signalled that we were ready to set sail, although the boat did have a motor we could use as well if time became of the essence. Eli had lined up a couple of other items to film this day.

We hopped aboard and lifejackets were offered. Hanchar had one on, but Eli and I declined, knowing where they were stowed if needed. With Hanchar at the rudder, we set out into the lake toward where the trio had their sighting seven months prior.

Venturing out onto the lake under nothing but the power of the wind and sails was a calming experience. Without the sound of a motor, and just the quiet wisp of the wind, I almost forgot we were there to work and in search of a monster people had been seeing for hundreds of years.

This adventure also marked the first time I'd ever been on the lake itself. All the times I'd visited Kelowna over the years I'd only once swam in it during a break from a day of mountain biking, and even then, only briefly. Being on the water now, I peered over the side of the boat while Eli, Hanson and Germaine chatted. What if there really was something down there, swimming beneath the surface, watching us pass by? I suddenly felt like that younger version of myself floating on the windsurf board on Shuswap Lake.

I still wasn't convinced a creature like Ogopogo could exist. However, the research I'd done so far did have me certain of two things: first, if Ogopogo was real, it wasn't anything like the marketing tool the region had cooked up to sell T-shirts and postcards. It was something to be taken seriously. Second, if it was real, it wasn't some fearsome beast either. If the four of us ended up in the drink, for whatever reason, Ogopogo wasn't going to come up from the depths to get us.

The location where their encounter took place was about thirty-five minutes from shore by sail and pretty much smack dab in the middle of the lake, south of the bridge where Highway 97 connected West Kelowna to Kelowna proper. Seeing something like Ogopogo in a place where skyscrapers and lakeside homes were still visible added a bit of an eerie quality to our trip. Monsters are supposed to live in remote places and to encounter one in such an urban setting felt off.

Which isn't to say I doubted Hanson, Hanchar, and Germaine's story. I didn't doubt for a second that they believe they saw something. Having hunted for ghosts in people's homes and within buildings in the middle of a town or city I should have known better than to feel this way. Strange things can appear in the most mundane of places.

Hanchar mentioned at certain times of year the lake is prone to the risk of driftwood – logs and large bits of trees or shrubs floating in the lake – which can pose a risk to unwary boaters. This is also what some skeptics chalk Ogopogo sightings up to.

"But driftwood bobs up and down in the water. It moves," Hanchar said. "What we saw wasn't moving. It just stayed still, like it was looking at us."

He said what appeared to be a long neck stretched deep into the water, out of sight. Yes, it could have been an uprooted tree in the water but, again, it wasn't moving. Whatever they took a picture of was stationary.

As if on cue, Hanson pointed deeper into the lake. Something was on the surface, almost at the point of our destination. Eli and I trained our cameras in that direction.

"See, it's driftwood," Hanchar said, and pointed.

Sure enough, what looked like several logs of varying size floated in the water. We sailed past several small ones, about the size of branches. There were bits of debris everywhere.

We cruised into the exact spot where Hanchar, Hanson and Germaine had their sighting and Hanchar let us float. A gentle breeze slowly carried us across the water.

Eli readied his camera, as did I. He wanted to cover the interview from multiple angles so not one bit of the story was missed. Being on the water, in the spot where their sighting took place and the now infamous photograph was taken, made for the perfect location to have this story told.

What follows is a mix of the interview taken on the day Eli and I ventured onto the water with Hanchar, Hanson and Germaine and an interview I conducted with the couple a few months prior.

"I was saying I should have put my movie-star makeup on and my movie-star hair," Hanson joked as cameras started rolling.

There were five of us on the sailboat, crammed into a little sitting area at stern. Germain and Hanson sat on a row of bench seats across from Eli and I, the eastern shore of the lake behind them. Hanchar sat on the lip of the sailboat at the rear near the engine.

"So, what were you guys doing out here on that day?" Eli began the interview.

"What we're doing right now," said Hanchar.

"Just enjoying the lake," Germaine added.

Before we continued, Hanson provided a little back story on the day, which was October 15, 2022. Her mom had passed away the day before at the age of 96 and Hanson was understandably in mourning. In fact, she had little to no interest in being out on the water that day but convinced herself to go.

"I said 'Universe, give me something else to think about besides my mother's death'," she said.

"And we came out, and the sun was glistening on the water and for October, it was the last sail of the year."

"It was warm," Germaine continued.

"Warm and beautiful out here," said Hanson.

Again, not the kind of day one associates with having an encounter with a monster of any kind. Stormy seas and overcast skies, yes, but not a warm, sunny day. But, from my experience, this is the way these things usually happen.

"I was very thankful that we were out here," Hanson added. "And then, all of a sudden, we saw the thing in the water."

Something was in the water some sixty to seventy feet away from them and slowly getting closer. The first thing the trio saw were the nodules or prongs sticking out of the water which, given the classical description of Ogopogo, could have been the often-described horns.

"Which looked like seaweed," said Germaine. "But it's fresh water. Where would the seaweed come from?"

There was something beneath the "seaweed" that they couldn't really see due to the sun's glare on the water, said Germaine. They knew there was something there, but what?

Hanchar picks up the story, saying upon first pass whatever it was in the water looked like a dead head, or partially submerged log, but it wasn't moving.

"I didn't like the looks of it because it was a bit of a boating hazard," he said.

They sailed past the object and Hanchar decided they should turn around and take another look. Whatever it was they saw just didn't feel right, so he asked Hanson to get her camera ready. He wanted to take a picture of it.

Hanson took out her phone, opened the camera app and held it ready. Hanchar said they got to within twelve feet of the object when she took the picture.

"And we kept right on going," he said.

A sailboat can only go so fast, and, for whatever reason, Hanchar didn't want to linger too long. The weather on the day we went out with them, and the day the sighting took place, was very similar right down to the wind speed. We weren't moving fast on the day of the interview so if there was something in the water that day which wanted to give chase, it wouldn't take long for it to overtake the sailboat.

Hanson continued the story, saying she only took one picture of the object, which she now regrets.

"While we were very slowly moving past it, I could clearly see the rest of it under the water," she said. "It was one thing to see what was sticking up out of the water, but I saw, and you too Myrna because you were looking at the same time, I saw what appeared to be its body or neck or the rest of it under the water."

The picture taken, Hanchar steered the sailboat towards shore, adding everyone was shaken by what they'd seen, even though they really didn't get a good look at it until they viewed the picture once they were on dry land.

Germaine clarified, saying the glare of the sun on the water somewhat obscured the object from the naked eye. The phone's camera, however, cut right through the glare and gave them a clear look at what, to them, could be the head of Ogopogo.

"We were shocked, basically, because we couldn't figure out what the heck it was," said Germaine.

"Did it make a noise or anything like that?" I asked of the thing in the water.

No sound at all, the trio confirmed. Nor did it move. Hanchar said even a gentle wind will cause ripples on the lake surface, and those ripples will cause a dead head or log to slowly bounce up and down in the water, disappearing for a while beneath the surface and then slowly coming back up. This didn't bounce up and down at all.

"It just stayed stable," said Hanchar.

"Super still," Hanson added.

"Unless it's absolutely flat calm a dead head will always be bobbing (in the water)," said Hanchar.

That's what Hanchar thought they'd encountered at first – a dead head. Hence, he turned the sailboat around for another look, intent on marking it so other boats didn't collide with what he believed was a log. It quickly became clear to all three that that wasn't what they saw.

Eli wanted to know how big the creature was. Germaine held her hands about three feet apart, indicating the size of the head. Hanson believes the tips of the nodules or horns stuck a good three to four inches out of the water.

"To me it looked like horns and ears," she said.

The object didn't look like wood either. Germaine and Hanson believe the object was coated in skin.

Hanchar has spent a good portion of his life on the water and has seen many logs with the stump still attached floating upside down while boating. For a stump to have worn so much through erosion in the water or by rubbing on a beach to look like what they took a picture of is highly unlikely, he said.

"A root wad sticking out of the water, usually you see roots, you see clearly that it's a stump upside down, right?" he said. "That was not the case. Those two nodules are too symmetrical to be something like that."

If you look at the picture closely, it doesn't look like a stump, asserted Hanchar.

"You look real close. It's not a stump," he said. "I know people thought we PhotoShopped it, but we don't even know how to do that."

Eli and I agree. I've studied the picture several times and so has Eli and several others in the cryptozoology community. People have said it looks like Hanchar, Hanson and Germaine have taken a picture of an upside-down duck and even a swimming dog. I don't believe it looks like any of those things. To me, and Eli as well, it closely resembles the statue of Ogopogo in Kelowna's waterfront park.

There are other theories behind the sighting, one of which is dragon-boat races used to be held on Lake Okanagan and one of the boats was lost to the lake. Eli asked the trio if that's what they might have seen?

Hanson said dragon boat races are still held on the lake. Hanchar asked if anyone knows of a dragon boat being sunk on the lake, adding they are valuable and, if one did sink, he believes the public would have heard about it.

"I'm sure someone would have salvaged it," said Hanchar. "And dragon boats don't have a head like that on them."

This is a valid point.

Given the size of what is believed to be the head, the rest of the animal they saw would have to be quite large as well, said Hanchar. His comment supports what others have claimed during alleged Ogopogo sightings – that the creature is large and long.

Hanchar continued the story, saying when he and Hanson got home, he jumped on the computer and checked the depth of the lake where they had their sighting. The location – the very spot where we now floated during this interview, is more than two hundred feet deep. There's no way what they saw could have been a large tree lodged in the bottom of the lake, or milfoil, a freshwater aquatic plant.

Given the time of year of their sighting, late October, there were no other boats on the water, said Hanson. In fact, theirs was the only vessel out at that time.

"It was so quiet," she said. "Maybe that's why we saw it? It's more prone to be seen when there aren't speedboats going around and there aren't so many people on the lake that it gets scared and goes down low?"

Other times of the year, especially July and August, the lake is a zoo, especially in the spot where the sighting occurred, said Hanchar. There are at least two marinas in the area and many private docks and boat launches. This could explain why they hadn't seen anything on the lake prior.

"We don't even boat here unless it's a day like when we went out in October," he said. "Not too many people are out swimming or waterskiing then."

This is a sound theory, as it would make sense such a creature would avoid noise and crowds. As has already been chronicled in this book, some Ogopogo sightings do take place in front of large groups of people, but it would make sense that the creature is a solitary one that wouldn't appear in too crowded and noisy an environment.

"What did you guys know about Ogopogo before you guys saw what you saw?" Eli asked.

Germaine had heard the many stories and rumors about a monster living in Lake Okanagan, saying the stories have been told forever. Hanchar agreed, adding anyone can go online and look up the stories and pictures associated with the legend.

He added that wakes from different boats travelling on different parts of the lake will eventually collide, causing disturbances on the water. From his experience these double wakes could be mistaken for Ogopogo, given the stories.

Hanchar went online after their sighting and looked at the various pictures of Ogopogo. As with Eli and I, he found the Soelin statue shared a likeness with what he saw in the water that October day.

"Why would they put horns on it? If this thing was like a snake or a reptile… horns?" he wondered aloud.

I pointed out the classic description of Ogopogo has the body of a serpent, the head of a horse or a dragon, and the tale of a whale. A dragon has horns on its head, much like the ones depicted in Soelin's statue. As mentioned previously in this book, other lake and sea monster sightings have a similar likeness.

Hanchar smiled and nodded his head. "Someone has obviously seen it to put horns on the one downtown," he said. "And there's other pictures you'll see where it has horns and ears. What did we see? Horns sticking up."

Hanson graduated high school in Kelowna during the 1970s, and she remembers she and her friends spent a lot of time at the beach. Her friends either claimed to have seen Ogopogo or heard stories about it.

"As kids we all talked about it, we were all aware there was some kind of a sea monster, or at least there was rumors of it," she said. "It's just a known Okanagan thing. It brings tourists here to learn about it or even see it.

"Who knows, maybe we'll even see it today?"

At that, we all kind of laughed but I know Eli and I took a quick glance at the water around us. Even if Ogopogo is friendly, one can't help but feel out of their element floating atop more than two hundred feet of water, an environment we are not genetically designed for. One can't help but feel a little vulnerable.

Hanchar echoed my sentiments. "If so, I just hope he's a fish eater," he said, causing us all to laugh. After showing a friend their photo, the friend vowed to never swim in Lake Okanagan again.

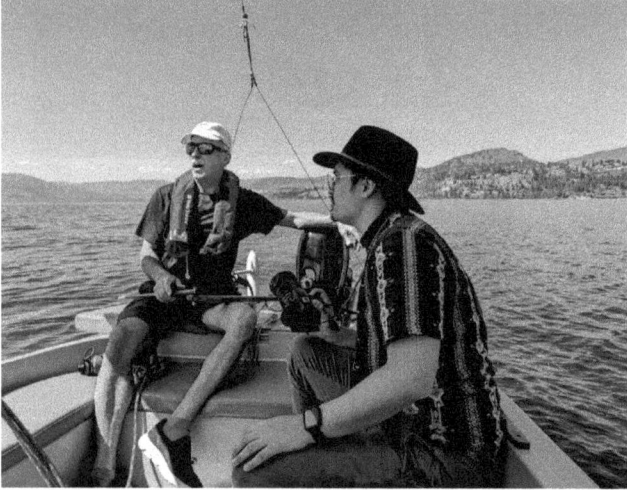

Watson interviews Hanchar

He wondered aloud if there's ever been a human-Ogopogo encounter. Aside from the McDougall story, there haven't been any aggressive Ogopogo sightings that any of us had heard. According to Hanchar, this suggests that, if there is a monster in Lake Okanagan, it sticks to a steady diet of fish. This supports information Gerhard provided earlier in this book.

Their sighting took place in October, at the tail end of the annual salmon spawning run in British Columbia, he said. Perhaps they saw Ogopogo as it surfaced to feed on the bounty of fish in the lake at that time of year?

Which begs the question: if Ogopogo were a flesh and blood creature, could it possibly be a species that journeys into Okanagan Lake – and possibly other area lakes as well – from the Pacific Ocean using various rivers and creeks? Or even a set of underground tunnels, which we'll touch on later in this book?

Hanchar said there are several creeks that drain into Lake Okanagan, including Mission Creek and Trust Creek. Checking Google Maps, there's also the Okanagan River, which is a tributary of the Columbia River, which runs into the Pacific Ocean. So, in theory, a creature like an Ogopogo could migrate, for lack of a better word, from the Pacific Ocean into Lake Okanagan as well as make the return trip. This could explain the limited number of sightings and monster hunters' inability to track down a carcass. It could also suggest the species of aquatic creature people have identified as the Cadborosaurus and Ogopogo are one and the same.

Still, you'd think we'd see these creatures in area rivers, and that one would even become trapped in the shallower water as salmon do every fall during their annual run, wouldn't you?

We continued floating and Hanson continued the story. When they returned to shore, they pondered what it was they had witnessed in the water.

"Wow, I said a prayer about that. Give me something to distract me from being not in the mood to be on the boat," she remembered thinking to herself. "Then I looked at this picture and I was like 'That is how big God is.' He, she, it – whatever it is – produced the Ogopogo. That was amazing."

Even being a non-religious person myself, the spiritual significance of Hanson's statement is a powerful one. If Ogopogo is more of a supernatural being, as First Nations claim, Hanson, Hanchar and Germaine's encounter certainly fits into the spiritual realm. Could *N'ha-a-itk* have appeared to give Hanson a temporary respite from her grief and depression? Possibly. One could also argue a series of random occurrences and a mistaken piece of floating debris played a trick on her subconscious desire for a moment of peace as well. The part of me who wants to believe in such things as Ogopogo finds such thoughts cynical but also possible.

Hanchar explained why they turned to Global News, a local television broadcaster, with the story. Being puzzled with what they'd taken a picture of, he decided to inform the media. However, the weekend the picture was taken coincided with a civic election in Kelowna, so it took several days for a journalist to get in touch with him.

By then, Hanson had gone to Alberta to attend her mom's memorial service. In the end, Hanchar and Germaine did the television news interview a few days later. It was that interview that gave the photograph worldwide attention.

"Why I wanted to go on Global was, if this was something somebody put in the water, whatever it was, it looked pretty solid. It created a water hazard. And, if it washed up on shore, on the beach or something, that I'd like to know," said Hanchar.

"What was it?"

He noted that he never once referred to what they took a picture of as Ogopogo during the television interview. His concern was something in the water that could be a hazard to boaters.

He and Hanson are also mystified at comments made by Adam Benedict, a folklore expert interviewed for the story, who believes the trio actually took a picture of a waterfowl like a duck. Hanchar would like to know why the media would include such a statement in the story, pointing out most of the comments that accompanied the story when it was posted to YouTube mocked Benedict and not them.

As a former newspaper reporter, I understand how news stories work. Journalists are supposed to get at least two sides to a story – a main opinion and an opposing view if you will – so it makes sense that the reporter sought out someone like Benedict. However, looking at Hanson's picture a lot during our time in Kelowna, Eli and I agree Benedict's assessment of what Hanchar and Hanson photographed is wrong. That is not a picture of a duck or other waterfowl.

In the days that followed, Hanchar, Hanson and Germaine watched the news for any update on their sighting, but nothing washed ashore. Nor has anything since then.

"It's pretty weird," said Hanson.

Suddenly, something to his left caught Hanchar's eye. Behind Eli and me.

"Look at this here," he said.

Something solid stuck out of the water, almost like a head.

"What am I looking at?" asked Eli.

"It's sticking up there," said Germaine, who lifted her sunglasses from her eyes to get a better look.

It was a dark shape, and quite a distance away. With nothing immediately beside it, it was hard to tell how big the something was.

"If we wanted to go turn around to explore what this is, we couldn't just turn around," said Hanson. "We'd have to move the sails."

Clearly, in a boat like theirs, a quick investigation isn't in the cards, which explains why they didn't go back for another look at the thing they took a picture of on that October day.

We continued along, staring at the object. It soon became clear that what we were looking at was a stick bobbing slowly up and down in the chop. Hanchar said they get a lot of such debris at this time of year as the rivers and creeks that drain into the lake are running high from snowmelt.

Eli turned to me. "I think we can cut it," he said, indicating the interview was over.

The rest of the sail passed uneventfully, and we eventually made our way back to shore, nary a lake monster in sight. On the way back, Hanson mentioned the woman who cares for her and Hanchar's dog has an Ogopogo story of her own to share and asked if we would we like to hear it.

Of course, we would.

Hanson pulled out her cellphone and phoned Jackie Michaud, asking her if she'd be okay with being interviewed for our project. Michaud agreed and, while Hanchar and Germaine secured the sailboat at the dock, Hanson followed Eli and I to my truck and navigated us to her home, where Michaud had just finished grooming the family dog.

Michaud is a pleasant, soft-spoken woman dressed in a button-up shirt adorned with pictures of dogs-fitting given her chosen profession. Hanson led us to her back deck, which provided perfect lighting for an interview with just enough shade to protect us from the sun that by now had reached the high point of the day. It was unseasonably hot. I didn't know about Eli, but I was missing the cool breeze that came from being on a sailboat.

Eli got Michaud set up with a microphone and readied his camera while I stood back to take notes. When she was comfortable, we began the interview.

It was the summer of 1977, July or August, and Michaud was sitting at Manhattan Beach in the north end of Kelowna with her sister and neighbour. She remembered it was early, about 7:30 in the morning.

"The lake was like glass. It was beautiful," she said.

Suddenly they noticed ripples in the water coming towards them, like a little wave. She remembered this being strange to the three of them because the water was otherwise perfectly still.

"It must be just an undercurrent," she thought at the time.

At first, she thought it was a SCUBA diver surfacing right in front of them, because the skin was black – maybe dark green – and rubbery looking, she said. It didn't take long for her to realize this was no SCUBA diver.

The three of them watched as the shape slipped back beneath the surface. It then swam down the lake away from them, its serpentine form undulating up and down in the water, surfacing for a moment or two and then disappearing underwater, only to repeat the process.

Giving themselves a few minutes to digest what they saw, the girls did what anyone would do after witnessing something like that – they phoned the local radio station.

"We think we just saw Ogopogo," Michaud told the person who answered the phone, and relayed her story.

Watson interviews Michaud

Surprisingly, theirs was not the only Ogopogo sighting to be reported to the radio station that day.

Someone else believed they'd spotted the elusive lake monster just two miles up the lake from where Michaud, her sister, and neighbour had their sighting.

A journalist with the radio station contacted Arlene Gaal about Michaud's sighting. Michaud had agreed to share her phone number with Gaal, who phoned her. The three girls visited Gaal at her home and shared their encounter, which Gaal documented for her records.

"She was awesome," Michaud said of her meeting with Gaal. "She was very knowledgeable."

Like Hanson and anyone else who grew up in Kelowna, Michaud had heard stories about Ogopogo all her life. When she and her friends would waterski, they'd quietly be afraid of falling lest they meet Ogopogo in the water while waiting for the boat to come back around.

"It was something we'd always heard about," said Michaud. "But that was my first and only encounter with it. It was pretty exciting!"

More than four decades have passed since Michaud's sighting, and she's never stopped believing in the Ogopogo. So many people in the region believe they've seen something. The more such stories she heard, the more credible the lake monster became, she explained.

She's seen Hanson and Hanchar's picture, and there's no doubt in her mind that they captured the lake monster in their photograph.

We wrapped up our interview and said goodbye to Michaud and Hanson, agreeing this had been a morning well spent. Not only did we have a couple of compelling interviews but were also able to spend some time on the lake itself, which was a real treat.

Eli had lined up an interview with Andrew McKay of *Into the Portal* podcast next, but we had a couple of hours to kill before meeting him. We decided to head downtown, grab some lunch, and then look for some Ogopogo swag. My son would definitely like an Ogopogo stuffy to add to his collection.

The traffic was bumper to bumper as we drove downtown and made our way to the park, where I opted to leave the truck while we ate and shopped. It was a Friday and school was still in session, but you'd swear it was a summer holiday weekend. Such is life in a tourist destination, I supposed.

Lunch was purchased at an American style barbecue restaurant, which I'm sure made Eli feel right at home. My goal was to get him a Tim Horton's coffee and breakfast the next morning. No one has truly visited Canada until they've had a large double-double coffee – as in two creams and two sugars – from Tim Horton's, which is our national chain coffee shop. The barbecue was delicious, however, and I don't think either of us realized how hungry we were until we actually sat down to eat.

We debriefed on the morning and agreed it went better than we could have hoped. Having the lake as our backdrop for Hanson and Hanchar's interview would play great on film, and their story, and Michaud's was compelling.

The more we discussed it, the more we became convinced they'd taken a picture of the lake monster.

Lunch accomplished, we ventured out in search of Ogopogo swag, stopping at a touristy shop we'd eyeballed the night before driving back from our trip to the park. The long, narrow shop was stacked with shirts, hats, keychains, postcards, and every manner of items you'd expect to find in such a store. Many had amusing sayings on them or showed off the many scenic sights one can visit in Kelowna, from wineries to the lakeside park just down the road.

And yes, a lot featured the cute, cartoon rendition of the Ogopogo. He appeared on everything from shirts to postcards, keychains, and wallets. There were also several sizes of smiling Ogopogo stuffed animals, one of which I grabbed for my son.

To my surprise, Eli grabbed one too.

"Who's that for?" I asked.

"Me."

"Really?"

"Heck yeah, dude! Who wouldn't want one." That last bit wasn't a question, but a statement.

"Valid point."

We spent a good thirty or so minutes wandering the shop before making our purchases. The place had a steady stream of people wandering in and out, many of whom made purchases like ours. More than a couple walked out with something related to Ogopogo.

Back outside, Eli asked for a time check. We still had about an hour to burn before meeting with Andrew, so Eli suggested we head back to the park. We'd spotted a visitor's centre the night before and decided that would be our next stop.

Navigating our way through the crowded sidewalk, I again marvelled at how busy this city is, how reliant on tourism it is, and how connected something like a lake monster is to that tourism brand. Probably even more so than Nessie to Loch Ness.

That last thought was cemented as soon as Eli and I stepped into the visitor's centre. There were even bigger Ogopogo stuffed animals. Displayed more prominently, however, was a series of children's books featuring the Ogopogo, or Ogie, as the lovable creature is often referred to in these books. The series has Ogopogo meeting mysterious strangers, saving busloads of stranded children, or highlights a boy's chance encounter with the lake monster, which prompts him to learn the First Nations legend behind the sightings.

Researching this latter book, a couple of months later, I learned the author, Dorothy Hawes, was encouraged not to publish the books by First Nations Chief Byron Lewis. In an interview with CBC News, Lewis claimed the book misappropriates his people's culture, beliefs, and structures.

Those very thoughts crossed my mind as I stared at the display of books and stuffed animals. I'd already spoken with Coralee Miller about this very thing and suddenly felt bad about buying my son a stuffed toy. All the years I'd visited Kelowna and studied Ogopogo, I'd never realized just how far tourism had taken the stories away from their roots.

Eli and I had been in Kelowna less than twenty-four hours, but already it was very clear to me that despite the best efforts of Tourism Kelowna, the monster alleged to be in Lake Okanagan is a far cry from the dopey character in books and on T-shirts and postcards. It might not be a fearsome beast, but it certainly isn't a children's story either.

Caught On Camera

Andrew McKay lives in a little West Kelowna apartment building with his wife, Amber Rae, and their dog. By little, we're talking maybe five hundred square feet; barely enough room for the three of them, at least by my estimation. There's all the necessary furniture a couple needs to live with, plus shelves of books, movies, and paranormal memorabilia.

He and Rae host the paranormal podcast *Into the Portal*, which launched in 2018. The couple cover a wide range of topics, from monsters and historical mysteries to Fortean legends and other high strangeness. Eli met McKay and Rae via an interview *Cryptid Campfire* did with the couple a few years prior. The topic, of course, was Ogopogo, and Eli was thrilled when McKay agreed to come on this documentary and talk about the lake monster.

McKay greeted us in the parking lot, right after an embarrassing – but successful – attempt to park my rather large truck in a small car parking stall. The first thing I noticed when meeting McKay is his positive energy. He immediately welcomed us and led us up to his apartment, talking energetically the entire way. Within minutes we were seated inside this air-conditioned space, an ice-cold glass of water in hand.

"So, what do you want to do the interview on?" he asked, adding he's willing to discuss pretty much anything related to Ogopogo.

What Eli was most interested in, and what McKay had previously promised he could deliver, is a trip to the spot where the Folden Film was shot in 1968. All that most people know is it was shot somewhere along Highway 97 between Kelowna and Penticton, the next major centre to the south.

"You bet!" he said and slapped the dinner table for emphasis. "Should we go do the interview there?"

Eli and I agreed that would be perfect, and minutes later we were in McKay's hatchback navigating through West Kelowna and onto Highway 97. Eli and McKay caught up, as they'd never met face to face before while I rested comfortably in the back.

Just beyond a turnoff that would have taken us west towards the Pacific Ocean, McKay slowed slightly and pointed towards a rapidly approaching side road.

"There. That looks like it," he said.

He signaled and turned off the highway onto the road. We drove a few metres and pulled off, Lake Okanagan to our right, and got out of the car. Eli handed McKay a mic and he and I readied our cameras. It was showtime once again.

Confusion was apparent on Eli's face when he couldn't pick up a signal from Andrew's lapel microphone. Then he realized he never turned it on and laughed. With a flick of a switch there was sound once again.

"This would be the best shot of Rattlesnake (Island) right here," said McKay.

"We'll get a shot of that," Eli said, zooming in on Ogopogo's alleged home. We would visit there in less than twenty-four hours.

Then Eli asked McKay to introduce himself and the interview began.

McKay explained we were in the rough vicinity of where the Folden Film was shot, maybe just a bit lower geographically as the road we currently stood on likely wasn't there in 1968. Looking through the trees, our view was very much that of the frame that potentially captured the sixty-foot-long lake monster.

"He essentially captured footage of an undulating, serpent-like object that seems to be surfacing and submerging at a pretty high rate of speed through the water," McKay said, explaining the footage Folden shot.

"The footage was obviously taken several decades ago. It's grainy and stuff like that. It's been edited and worked with a number of times but that's essentially what it shows."

Although it's never been proven that Folden caught the Ogopogo on camera, the film is the first such record of the creature. In the late 1940s or early 1950s there was a photo taken of what was believed to be Ogopogo on the beach on the east side of the lake, said McKay. In addition to the photograph, this sighting was witnessed by several people.

"Like double digits of witnesses who saw essentially the same thing as what Folden caught on film. Essentially a serpent-like creature, but much closer to shore," he said.

Scrolling through Bill Steciuk's website sometime later, I come across two such sightings that could be the one McKay is talking about. In 1926, about thirty cars along Okanagan Mission Beach, which is on the side of the lake McKay mentioned, reported seeing Ogopogo. Then, in 1947, several boaters all saw the creature at the same time. One described it as having a "long sinuous body, about thirty feet in length, consisting of about five undulations, apparently separated from each other by about a two-foot space, in which part of the undulations would be underwater. There appeared to be a forked tail, of which only one half came out of the water. From time to time the whole thing submerged and came up again."

McKay said the different sightings decades apart had him speculating if there is more than one Ogopogo and if these creatures are of a different size.

Eli agreed, saying he recalls a sighting where the witness believed he or she saw a whole family of Ogopogos at the same time. McKay said there's been a few incidents where multiple lake monsters have been seen at the same time.

He recalled the story of an avid swimmer who took off from a beach on his regular swimming route, which was close to Bertram Creek Park one day.

"He reported being pursued or being followed by multiple creatures, I believe three, and they were on the smaller side," said McKay. "He ended up speculating, I think if my memory serves me correctly, that they might have been juvenile Ogopogos, which is fascinating."

Eli remembered this story and jumped in with the swimmer's name: Daryl Ellis. Some further research expands the story: Ellis was a marathon swimmer back in 2000 and he swam the full length of Lake Okanagan to raise money for cancer research. He claimed two creatures followed him from beneath the surface, and quietly called to his spotter boat, which came and collected him. A few minutes passed with no further sign of anything in the water, so Ellis dived back in and resumed his swim. As he swam by Rattlesnake Island, he said the creatures returned and followed him for several minutes before disappearing from view again. According to Ellis' report, one creature was twenty- to thirty-feet-long while the other appeared somewhat smaller. Later, as he swam near the lake's floating bridge, Ellis believed another monster appeared within nine metres of him. This one had eyes the size of a grapefruit.

While we had McKay, Eli decided to pick his brain on a few other things Ogopogo related. He asked if McKay could flesh out any details regarding Susan Allison, who you'll recall is the first European settler to report seeing Ogopogo.

"Susan Allison is such a cool angle to the Ogopogo story because of how early she was here," said McKay.

Her house still stands and is a part of Quail's Gate Winery, he said. Anyone can go and visit the home. McKay continued, saying Allison's husband had a close encounter with Ogopogo, but little is known about what transpired. Allison had befriended many of the Indigenous people of the area and had heard all the stories and legends.

"She was a firm believer in it (Ogopogo) and when she published her autobiography there was reference to the creature in it," McKay said. "It's one of the first officially published references to Ogopogo."

We paused and looked at the stand of trees nearby, the lake visible behind it with Rattlesnake Island in the distance. Eli commented on how where we were standing was very "Folden Filmish" and McKay and I agreed. McKay pointed out how the lake is so narrow and how the wind funnels through the valley which, along with all the boat traffic, creates anomalous waves. Several such waves moved about the lake while we watched, and there were no boats present to cause them.

"Someone who is not necessarily researching Ogopogo but has heard the stories can look down and find some sort of wave and undulation that is coming from nothing in the water," McKay said, adding this leads them to believe they've seen the lake monster.

"I love that because it leads to more people having an interest in the subject. It almost adds a layer of camouflage for the actual creature itself."

Which begs the question: has McKay ever seen Ogopogo?

"I've definitely seen things in the water that I can't explain," he said. "I've never seen an actual firm solid object like something on the Folden Film, but I've definitely seen things that, at first, I thought was something like an anomalous wave, but, on close inspection or watching for longer, it seemed like something much stranger."

Whenever he's on the lake, be it paddle boarding with Rae or swimming, the possibility of an Ogopogo encounter is constantly on his mind, he said. This always leaves him a little spooked, largely because of the John McDougall story where McDougall and his boat were almost pulled down into the depths in the middle of the lake.

"If you already have a little bit of a fear of deep water, that's definitely going to be spooky if you're out there paddle boarding on Okanagan Lake," said McKay.

This despite the consensus from researchers and First Nations that whatever Ogopogo is, it's a peaceful and benevolent creature with little interest in harming anyone, he said.

The McDougall story does remain the scariest Ogopogo story, and McKay launched into it at Eli's request. As previously mentioned in this book, McDougall was trying to cross the lake with his horses at a time long before there was a bridge or ferry. The only real option was to swim the horses across or a take a barge.

McDougall opted to swim the horses across, the ropes tethered to them from his canoe which he paddled, said McKay. He encountered something on the lake that took hold of a couple of horses and dragged them under.

"Nobody knows what the fate of every creature involved in that case was," said McKay. In the end,

McDougall cut the ropes attached to the horses to avoid being pulled into the depths himself.

"That story is definitely the most grim of Ogopogo stories."

The story also begs the question of why a generally harmless creature would engage in such a violent and deadly act? Was it being territorial? Did McDougall fail to take the lake monster stories seriously and pay the price? Things to ask Coralee Miller when we spoke to her the following day.

"That led into beliefs that you need to appease the creature or provide offerings. Things like that," McKay said. "I don't know for how long early settlers and pioneers played into those narratives, but it was probably worth a try when going across (the lake) a second time."

Our time with McKay was almost up, so Eli wanted to know his thoughts on *Ogopogo Quest*, Bill Steciuk's passion project when it comes to Ogopogo. McKay said the site is a "wealth of information" when it comes to anything and everything related to Ogopogo, and he and Rae referenced it heavily during their *Into the Void* episodes on the lake monster.

The interview over, Eli focused his camera on Rattlesnake Island and marvelled at how small it is. McKay said it is much bigger when you are close to it, something Eli and I would experience soon enough.

We then dropped McKay off at his apartment and decided to head to Quail's Gate Winery so we could get a look at Susan Allison's abode.

The drive to Quail's Gate afforded us views of green, rolling hills, the blue water of the lake, and long stretches of vineyards from where future bottles of wine would be created. We soon arrived at our destination and made our way into the tasting room, which was packed with people shopping for and sampling wines. Many were dressed to the nines, which suddenly made Eli and I – dressed in jeans, boots, casual shirts, and our trademark cowboy-style hats – stand out.

We quickly sought out an employee, which was easy to find given they all wore shirts carrying the Quail's Gate logo. Eli mentioned we were looking for Susan Allison's house and, instead of getting a weird look, the employee smiled and directed us across the property.

"It's an old log house. You can't miss it," she said.

Indeed, we couldn't. The logs have long since been dyed grey and black by years in the elements, but Susan Allison's home is very well preserved. It was closed at the time of Eli's and my visit, but we were able to peer inside and see how it currently serves as a market for Kelowna and Okanagan-based artisans. Displays of weaving, paintings, pottery, and photography were visible through the panes of glass, creating the picture of a cozy environment for artisans to work.

The lawn outside the home is decorated with several picnic tables, creating an almost park-like environment for people to enjoy a nice lunch during the spring, summer, and fall. And yes, the lake is a short distance away, so seeing a lake monster, especially back at a time when there was less infrastructure to disturb the view, doesn't seem out of the question.

Author outside of Susan Allison's home

Eli shot some footage of the home while I wandered outside. Some research revealed John and Susan Allison built their small log cabin in 1873 and made it their home until 1881. The Allisons' ranching life began in Princeton, a couple of hundred kilometres to the southwest, but they drove their head of cattle to the Okanagan for winter grazing. The cabin's location is on the sunny side of the lake, to use Allison's words, at the base of Mount Boucherie.

The property was sold to a John Davidson in 1881 and changed hands several times in the ensuing decades. When Quail's Gate took ownership, the home served as the wine shop from 1990 to 2006 before it became the Allison House Market.

What's not mentioned in the history provided by Quail's Gate and other standard historical documents is the lake monster sighting that brought us here. I wondered if that staff member would have been so forthcoming in directing us to it if she'd known we were filming an Ogopogo documentary?

What is mentioned in most of the records that Eli and I uncovered is slight. The sighting occurred in 1873, and Allison claimed she saw a snake-like creature moving through the water. Andrew McKay provided more details than most of the accounts we read.

The afternoon shadows were growing long, and the temperature kept climbing. It was unseasonably hot out and neither Eli nor I was dressed for the weather. We were sweating and tired and decided we'd shoot some quick B-roll along the lake before heading back to the hotel and calling it a day.

On the drive back we agreed it had been a successful first day of filming. A solid interview in the morning and an unexpected one right after. Plus, we not only found the location the Folden Film was shot but also got to visit Susan Allison's home as well. We called it a great start and agreed to meet for dinner after a bit of a rest and cool down.

That night's dinner consisted of burgers at Red Robin and our usual nightcap outside the hotel. I also received a bedtime phone call from my son, which was unusual. He was excited to tell me his last baby tooth had finally come out after what had been a struggle to remove it over several days.

"That's awesome buddy. You gonna leave it out for the tooth fairy?"

"Yup."

For the record, he's well aware the tooth fairy is his mom, but we still enjoy playing make believe.

We said our love you's and goodbyes and ended the call. Then it hit me; I missed the moment his last baby tooth came out. A moment that could never be recaptured or experienced again.

This wasn't the only such moment I'd missed as a father either. Back in 2012, when I was one half of the pop-culture podcast *From the Basement*, I travelled to Montreal to cover a film shoot starring Fred "The Hammer" Williamson and *Arrow in the Head* founder John Fallon. I even got to play an evil henchman who is killed in the movie during a shootout. It was a great time, and I had a lot of fun. Something I'll never forget.

While I was having fun on the other side of Canada my son took his first steps. I wasn't there for that either.

The pursuit of our passions can lead us astray from the things that really matter sometimes, and I walked back into the restaurant melancholic. Eli picked up on that right away and asked what was wrong, so I told him.

"Oh man. How do you feel about that?"

"I don't know, Eli. I don't know."

The next morning came quickly enough, and Eli and I met once again in front of the truck, our equipment packed and ready. With another scorcher of a day ahead I opted to wear shorts. Eli stuck with pants for the simple reason he didn't anticipate such weather in Canada and didn't pack anything for hot weather.

The first order of the day was breakfast, and I promised Eli no trip to Canada was complete without breakfast at Tim Hortons.

For the uninitiated Tim Hortons – aka Tim's, Timmie's or Timmie Hortons – is a chain of donut and coffee shops that's Canada's equivalent of Dunkin' Donuts. The name comes from its founder, Tim Horton, who was a National Hockey League player from 1949 until his death in an automobile accident in 1974. Given Canada's love of hockey, Tim Hortons is a Canadian institution and the best way to make Eli an honorary Canadian was to take him there for coffee and breakfast.

As luck would have it, there is a Tim Hortons directly across the parking lot from the Sncewips Heritage Museum in West Kelowna where we were to meet with Coralee Miller and her co-worker and cousin, Kayt Ell. So, we put the address into Google Maps and made our way there in record time.

The Tim Hortons staple is what us Canucks call a large double-double, which is a large coffee with two hits of cream and two scoops of sugar, so I insisted Eli have one of those with a breakfast wrap. I ordered the same.

We grabbed our trays of food and sat down. I watched as Eli unwrapped his breakfast wrap and took a bite. He chewed for a bit and nodded his head.

"It's not bad. Not bad."

I agreed. This is fast food not gourmet food. "Now wash it down with some coffee."

The one problem with Tim Hortons is sometimes the coffee comes warm and sometimes it comes scalding hot. With the sleeves on the cardboard mugs, it can be hard to tell. Eli took a big hit of coffee, and it was immediately clear he got the scalding hot.

"Oh," he exclaimed. "That's hot!"

He wisely decided to let the coffee cool before having any more and we worked out some interview questions while we ate, customers coming and going all the while.

One approached Eli during a napkin run, saying he'd watched Eli on the Small Town Monsters YouTube channel and liked his work. He was on his way to a Bigfoot conference in Merritt, the first of its kind in the Interior of British Columbia, and we all ended up talking Sasquatch for a few minutes before the guy snapped a quick selfie with Eli and hit the road. We decided to head across the parking lot to meet Miller and Ell.

Miller was waiting for us at the museum entrance, and, it must be said, the museum itself is not what I expected. It's an actual storefront in the middle of a strip mall, all modern cream-colored walls and shiny glass. The exhibits of Westbank First Nations history and culture stand out against the modern design, the masks, artwork, canoes, and varied artifacts beautifully on display.

Having "met" Miller virtually during our initial interview, I recognized her right away. Stocky with dark hair and glasses, her presence was even more welcoming in person. She has a sense of humor about things and that shines through in her demeanor, which is both professional and personable.

We shook hands and I introduced her to Eli, who did the same.

"This place is amazing," said Eli, taking in the displays that make up the museum's main room.

"Thank you," Miller said with a smile.

We decided on a spot to conduct the interview, which was at the back of the museum away from the eyes of any passersby. At that point Ell – a quiet blonde with the hint of an Irish accent – arrived and helped us set up, ensuring the museum door was locked so no one would come in and interrupt the interview.

What follows is a combination of my initial online conversation with Miller and our on-site interview.

So, what is Ogopogo to the Indigenous people of the Okanagan?

"We don't call it Ogopogo," said Miller. "That name, that whole entity, has been created by Kelowna."

Westbank First Nation has no issue with the Ogopogo brand or its use as a tourism draw, as Ogopogo is loved by so many people, said Miller. But she acknowledged that Ogopogo does do harm to the cultural significance of the water spirit *N'ha-a-itk*, which first appeared in her people's stories in the 1400s.

When broken down, *N'ha-a-itk* means inside, miraculous, wonderful, divine, and how the water moves.

Put these all together and you have the sacred spirit of the lake, she said. Despite what the Westernized version of the legend will tell you, *N'ha-a-itk* isn't some savage lake monster that needs to be appeased before venturing onto the water.

"It does not eat chickens or pigs," said Miller. "We definitely didn't feed it puppies or horses because that shit is expensive. That's like me rolling my Volvo into the lake and [saying] 'Hope you're happy'."

As a spirit of the lake, *N'ha-a-itk* does like tobacco, sage and to be sung to. Most importantly it wants to be clean, she said. So, prayers and blessings are made to *N'ha-a-itk*, but only as an offering of thanks.

The whole "flesh things" Miller said, referring to sacrificial references in the Ogopogo legend, came about quite by accident. Susan Allison was one of the first settlers to see the spirit of the lake, and it spooked her. The same reaction occurred among other settlers who lived on Lake Okanagan and caught a glimpse of *N'ha-a-itk*.

"They would freak out," said Miller.

This fear grew whenever settlers would see the Indigenous people place tiny slices of meat into the water. Miller said the settlers mistook this gesture to mean the "monster" was bloodthirsty and demanded a sacrifice be made.

"When we offer a little bit of meat to the water, it's never to appease the water spirit. It's an acknowledgement to what the water spirit gives us," she said. "Without clean water there are no plants, there is no travel, there are no fish. So, water represents all the blessings that sustain us."

First Nation culture is based on reciprocation. What is taken from the land must be given back, and that usually comes in the form of an act of service, said Miller. In modern times this includes prescribed burning, harvesting fruits and vegetables, scattering of seeds, and monitoring animals and livestock.

When it comes to a spirit like *N'ha-a-itk*, whatever is given to the spirit is returned to the people. If one enters the water with ill intentions or a poor, disrespectful attitude, the water will act accordingly in return, she said. Because Lake Okanagan has a lot of underwater caves and strong currents, behaving in a safe manner is a way to show respect to the water spirit.

Watson interviews Miller

In its spiritual form, Miller's elders say *N'ha-a-itk* has the body of a serpent, the head of a horse, and antlers of a deer, which isn't far from the description Tourism Kelowna adopted as its mascot, nor what Gerhard described as being seen in lakes all over the world.

However, and contrary to the hopes and dreams of cryptozoologists and monster hunters everywhere, *N'ha-a-itk*'s true form – the only one you can see and even touch – is the lake water itself, she said.

"You can't catch *N'ha-a-itk*. You can hold it in a cup but if you're hoping to drag ashore some kind of slithering beast, it's not going to happen," said Miller.

The same is true of Sasquatch or Bigfoot, as it's more widely known. For Indigenous people, Sasquatch isn't a flesh-and-blood man ape like many believe it to be. Miller said it's a spiritual being – a dimension walker – and if you see it, it's only because it wants you to.

If this isn't a flesh-and-blood creature, then what is it people are seeing on those rare occasions and why? If this is a spirit of the lake, then why see a sighting of something physically on or in the water?

Miller said those who witness *N'ha-a-itk* in its physical form are simply lucky.

"That or you're drunk. A lot of people like to boat with a brewski," she said jokingly, before getting serious again.

"If you happen to see it, enjoy it. If you try and tell people you've seen it, no one is going to believe you. And, for some reason, no one can keep their bloody camera still."

It's one thing to see *N'ha-a-itk*, or even Bigfoot, but it's another thing entirely to go in search of such spirits, and such a quest can come at a cost in the form of trouble for the seeker, she said. Spirits like *N'ha-a-itk* are private creatures who show themselves because they choose to. But to safely see one, there must be respect on the part of the person seeking it out.

"If you're going into the bush looking for *Stronitum* (Bigfoot); for one that's dangerous. And two, you better have the proper offerings," said Miller.

Her elders wander the woods with rocks in their pockets to give as an offering to Sasquatch. Miller said her people made a contract with Sasquatch stating if the two should meet, they would give Sasquatch a rock... and not just any pebble off the ground, but a rock that is special to you.

Miller explained further, saying Sasquatch used to babysit the Westbank First Nation children but that arrangement came to an end when Sasquatch began eating the young boys and girls. The Indigenous people cut ties with the forest spirit, which promised it would always keep a watchful eye on what the humans were up to. The gift of a personal rock guarantees safe passage in the woods.

Sasquatch also looks after her people's fish, with Coyote acting as a middleman of sorts. Coyote would ask how many fish the First Nations could harvest per season, and Sasquatch would provide an amount, said Miller.

Although not directly about *N'ha-a-itk*, learning about the relationship between Indigenous people and Sasquatch provides some understanding of their connection to the spirit of the lake as well, showing a reliance on such a being for their very lives. To disrespect that connection can spell trouble.

N'ha-a-itk lives on Rattlesnake Island, so named due to its snake population. Miller said *N'ha-a-itk* lives with the snakes because it has a close relationship with the land spirit, which is snake-like.

One can journey to Rattlesnake Island on a clear, calm day; but, if you haven't dropped tobacco or provided a song as a gift of respect to *N'ha-a-itk*, the water will soon get choppy and toss the boat or canoe about, said Miller.

"You need to have manners when going out onto the water," she said. "We're all connected by spirit, just not in form. Part of our teachings is human and nature are not two separate categories. We're one and the same."

As an example, she wouldn't walk into my home without knocking on the door first and asking for an invite. She said the same rules apply when venturing into the woods or onto a lake – you ask permission first.

"There has to be respect, there has to be sincerity, and there has to be good intentions behind your visit," said Miller.

"And the water spirit, I'm told, doesn't want to show itself because it's dirty. The cleaner the water the happier our spirit is."

Water is a sacred aspect in Indigenous culture. Her people begin life in the sacred waters of the womb, it connects people through travel, and it cleanses and heals their hearts and souls.

"If we're having a bad day, we're instructed to take it to the water because the water listens," said Miller. "Water teaches us to be mindful because, whatever we do upstream, it affects somebody downstream."

Sadly, people don't quite understand all this and, instead, only focus on the creature some believe they see on the lake. The very one also seen on postcards and that turns up in cryptozoology documentaries. In fact, back in the 1990s, the global environmental campaign network Greenpeace sent the City of Kelowna a petition to make Ogopogo a protected species. Politicians agreed, and, to this day, Ogopogo remains on the protected species list. Miller said this shows how people don't understand what *N'ha-a-itk* really is.

"When I go to the marsh, I'm still seeing beer cans and baby diapers floating in the water," she said. "You're missing the mark because the creature and the water are one and the same."

This begs the question, given how Western culture struggles to respect our environment, is there any animosity on the part of Indigenous people when it comes to not only our culture's treatment of the environment, but of *N'ha-a-itk*? Miller said such animosity does exist, but there also seems to be a fear on the part of Westerners towards the lake, be it borne out of a fear of water in general, or the fact a monster could be residing within.

Going into the water with that fear, or even a sense that one can claim dominion over nature, usually leads to nature humbling you in some way, she said. The best way to avoid such an outcome is, as Miller pointed out earlier, to show the water – and *N'ha-a-itk* – respect.

"The water is a living thing. Whether it has its spooky form, or it is just water, it's a part of you all the same," she said.

Obviously, I'm not the first paranormal investigator or cryptozoologist to ask Miller about *N'ha-a-itk*. She said most are not happy with what she has to tell them because they hope the likes of Ogopogo and Sasquatch are flesh-and-blood monsters that can be brought before a wall of television cameras as a way to show irrefutable proof such things exist.

If these monsters aren't monsters at all but spirits, well, how do you catch a spirit? Miller said you can't.

Continuing with that thought process, the very act of turning *N'ha-a-itk* into the tourism mascot Ogopogo has created a disconnect in people's minds. Miller said Western culture views Ogopogo as something like Santa Claus when, to her people, *N'ha-a-itk* is very real.

"It's not this derpy character that sells apples and jerky. This is our water spirit," said Miller.

Having seen the displays of Ogopogo stuffed animals and children's books and being guilty of purchasing one of the toys myself, I fully understood how Miller and other Westbank First Nations are disappointed by how an important part of their culture is misrepresented and even sold to unwitting tourists.

What's also sad is many Westbank First Nations have come to believe the tourism hype, right down to stories of Indigenous people making sacrifices to appease the fierce water spirit, she said.

So, when witnesses make their claims of seeing a monster on the lake, or photographs surface of something mysterious breaking the surface in a grainy photograph or blurry video, what goes through Miller's mind, and the minds of Westbank First Nations? Do they take these accounts as *N'ha-a-itk* making a rare appearance in its physical form, especially when the stories, videos and photographs attract often international media attention?

"I think it's funny," she said, adding it's considered taboo to even take pictures or video during ceremonies related to *N'ha-a-itk* and other spirits.

If one happens to be there on the very rare occasion when *N'ha-a-itk* does take to its physical form, put the damn camera away and be present, Miller said.

"Just sit and watch. How lucky if it truly is the water spirit," she said. "Or even if it's a big-ass sturgeon, still, that's cool. Just sit down and look at it.

"As long as you believe what you saw, let that feed you. I think people are trying to get rich from it and, if you go in with that kind of intention, it's going to backfire on you."

This might sound funny coming from someone who has documented cases of paranormal activity in the past, posted such videos to YouTube, and written about them in books, but I'm inclined to agree with Miller on this last point. Not enough merit is given to the personal experiences people have when it comes to the paranormal. Seeing a ghost or a Sasquatch is a rare and amazing experience, and it should be enough. But we often want that experience validated further by showing others through video and photographic evidence. Sadly, this often results in ridicule and claims we made the whole thing up. Perhaps such experiences should end with having the experience itself?

Miller said Westbank First Nations are brought up to believe that if they have a fantastical experience, then it's real. It doesn't have to be validated further.

"If you've read it in a book, it's not real," she said, and laughs.

To the monster hunters and cryptozoologists out there, who intend to come to Lake Okanagan with their boats loaded with side-scan sonar and their SCUBA gear to search the lake, or their DNA testing equipment, Miller said don't waste your time. All you will find with your scientific means of proving or disproving *N'ha-a-itk*'s existence is water.

"The water that takes on the spiritual form that people find," she said. "That's cool, but its true, true form is water."

And when people ask her how to catch Ogopogo?

"I'm like 'Here's a cup. Good luck'," she said.

Talking to Miller was a fascinating experience. Prior to talking to her, I'd begun to think of cryptids as being more than an unidentified species. Given the paranormal nature of many accounts, with Bigfoot tracks disappearing in the middle of a snow-covered field, I was leaning further away from the flesh-and-blood concept. Talking to her has helped me shift that thinking even more.

Looking at Eli as he conducted and filmed the interview, I saw a similar light go off in his eyes as well. Ever the professional, he continued his line of questions, inquiring into how the Okanagan region got its name.

European settlers were no strangers to the Westbank people as groups of hunters and explorers would travel into the area from the United States, said Miller. The first documented settler to trade with the population was David Stewart of the Northwest Company, a fur trading business headquartered out of Montreal, Canada, during the late 1700s.

Stewart eventually asked the Indigenous people who they were. Being the literal type, they took that to mean what they did, said Miller. This group was scouts, and they responded accordingly in their native tongue. Stewart started using the phrase to address other First Nations during his travels, horribly mispronouncing the word. This mispronunciation eventually became Okanagan.

"And that is how we got saddled with the name," she said. "This became the Okanagan Valley and we the Okanagan People."

Has Miller seen *N'ha-a-itk*? She has not. But she has felt its presence and behaves accordingly when venturing into or onto the lake.

"You always go into the water with respect," she said.

Just because someone doesn't see a horned serpent in the lake doesn't mean it can't make itself known in other ways. Miller said *N'ha-a-itk* can be seen in the way the sunlight reflects off the water, creating a serpentine reflection move across the lake.

The Okanagan Valley is known for its wind, which frequently whips along the lake's surface causing large waves to flail about. Miller said this makes many boaters and swimmers nervous but to her people, it brings comfort.

"When the water is choppy and flailing and rolling, that's when we know our water spirit is happiest. We consider it's playing," she said.

As for today's expedition, Miller said the weather is perfect for a trip to Rattlesnake Island. Whether we'll get close to *N'ha-a-itk*'s home or not is up to the water spirit. She and Ell will drop tobacco into the lake as an offering and introduce us. If *N'ha-a-itk* is agreeable we'll be able to pull right up to the island, and possibly even venture onto it.

"If the water starts to pick up and get choppy, not today," she said. "Today it's going to be a coin toss."

We wrapped up the interview and filmed some B-roll throughout the museum. We had about an hour to go before meeting Bill Steciuk and Olivier Asselin and knew traffic would be picking up as it was Saturday morning and people would be getting out to take advantage of the day.

Miller gathered several items to join us on our expedition to Rattlesnake Island, including drums and sage, which would be used as part of an offering we'll give to *N'ha-a-itk* to ensure safe passage to the island.

Given that Ell was with us, we extended the invitation to join us and were glad when she accepted. Minutes later we were in the truck and driving back to Hotel Eldorado for another trip onto the lake.

As we pulled into the parking lot, the same challenge as the previous day presented itself: where to park the damn truck? I love my Dodge but, at moments like this, I also missed my Honda Civic.

A ten-minute search and short walk later and we were heading toward the same marina we'd attended the day before. As if right on cue, my friend and colleague Olivier Asselin pulled in with a truck that, would you believe, is even bigger than mine! We said a quick hello, and I directed him to the same general vicinity of where I parked. With his drone and enthusiasm in hand, Asselin joined us as we made our way to the docks and Bill Steciuk.

The Trip to Rattlesnake Island

Bill Steciuk's search for the creature known as Ogopogo began in October of 1978 while driving across the floating bridge from West Kelowna when something on the north side of the lake caught his attention.

Swimming toward the main city of Kelowna were three small humps and what appeared to be a head.

Steciuk pulled over and got out of his car. He ran to the edge of the bridge and looked over, wanting to get a better look. This, of course, snarled traffic and caused other motorists to climb from their vehicles and look as well. Soon he was joined by twenty others who gazed at the object for the next sixty seconds before it disappeared beneath the surface, leaving a large wake on the water.

The sighting made a believer out of Steciuk, and he vowed on the spot to one day search for the creature full time. That opportunity presented itself twenty years later when he was joined by a sizable group who helped him mount an expedition to find the elusive lake monster in August of 2000.

Armed with high-tech sonar equipment donated by Interphase Technologies of Soquel, California, the search focused on Rattlesnake Island, where there are several large underwater caves where the monster is believed to reside, some of which had never been explored at that time.

On the eighteenth day of the search sonar picked up a fast-moving object about fifteen meters long travelling forty-eight metres in front of the boat in a part of the lake that was sixty-five metres deep. The sonar sweep lasted thirty-five seconds before the object moved away from the boat and dropped out of reach of the sonar.

This success prompted a second expedition in August of the following year. This time the team searched not only Rattlesnake Island but also an area north of Kelowna near a junction of water where several creeks run into Lake Okanagan, as many recent sightings of the time took place there. The team also focused on Seclusion Bay south of West Kelowna where many unexplained water disturbances and Ogopogo sightings have been reported.

Although several possible indications of a large creature were captured on sonar, none were as conclusive as the one recorded on the previous expedition.

Both expeditions were well documented in the media and put Steciuk on the map when it came to Ogopogo, earning him the title of the Legend Hunter. He's been featured in several documentaries and TV series about the elusive Ogopogo, including *MonsterQuest*. He also launched his *OgopogoQuest.com* site, which has already proven an invaluable tool while writing this book.

As you can see, Steciuk is the right man to take us to Rattlesnake Island, and we were all excited to meet one of the most respected Ogopogo researchers in the world.

Steciuk was waiting for us at the boat, which he'd secured and fuelled for us. Our goal was to interview

Steciuk, record a traditional Westbank First Nations offering to *N'ha-a-itk* to ensure safe travel, and hear many of the stories related to the island and the water spirit. Asselin and I also hoped to "touch down" on the island itself and explore it.

Walking to the marina, we soon realized we had no idea where Steciuk was and where we were supposed to meet him. I offered to start shouting "Bill" at the top of my lungs, but we quickly decided that would be unprofessional.

At first, we thought he would be waiting for us on the same docks we departed from the previous day. Then we clued in that he was in the actual marina where boats are rented from and made our way there with Eli in the lead.

"I feel weird with this crowd of people behind me," Eli said, and laughed.

"We're following you. You're our leader," I replied jokingly.

We all had a good chuckle as we approached the marina office. Eli asked the attendant if she knew if Steciuk was here, and she pointed to a large vessel around the corner. Sure enough, there he was.

Steciuk is about my height, so roughly six-feet-tall, and was dressed in jeans and navy-blue jacket atop of a collared shirt with nautical images on it. His ball cap also sported a naval symbol. He looked every part the boat captain he would be on this expedition.

Saying our hellos and shaking hands, Eli and Steciuk exchanged Release Forms allowing each other to use any footage for their own purposes. Apparently Steciuk intended to use this trip for his website, which we were all okay with. With the documents signed, we were ready to shove off.

But not before Miller and Ell said a quick prayer to the water asking it to take care of us. That done, the bow of the boat was pushed from the dock by the deck hands and Steciuk fired up the motor. We were on our way.

Miller provided us with individual packets of tobacco, so we each deposited them into the lake and introduced ourselves in turn, hoping this would guarantee us safe travels to Rattlesnake Island. The sudden change in velocity prompted Eli to remove his signature black cowboy hat as the first gust of wind nearly ripped it from his head.

The majority of us were seated at the bow, and Steciuk asked some of us to retreat to the stern to better shift the weight on the boat. Eli, Miller and I took our seats behind Steciuk and he shifted the engine to full throttle.

It's hard to communicate over the sound of the motor and the wind, so we sat in silence for a good portion of the journey. I'm not sure what was going through everyone's mind, but I was curious what – if anything – we might encounter at Rattlesnake Island. I knew Steciuk's expedition years before had turned up… something. Would we be so lucky? Did having Miller and her cousin with us increase our chances of an encounter? And, if *N'ha-a-itk* was indeed a water spirit, would it try to discourage our visit by a change in the weather and water?

Rattlesnake Island isn't just known for being the possible home of a legendary lake monster. In the 1970s the island belonged to Eddie Haymour, who dreamed of turning it into an Arabian-themed amusement park complete with mini-golf course, replica pyramids, restaurants, and a giant camel. Seeing the size of the island, it's hard to believe he would have fit all that on the relatively small land mass.

Suffice to say, the amusement park didn't happen. Haymour blamed the provincial government of the day, cooking up a conspiracy theory the government was out to get him. He had already begun construction, the remnants of which can still be seen on the island, but the province decided it didn't want a theme park on Rattlesnake Island. This prompted the Royal Bank to withdraw the loan it had given Haymour. The government offered to buy the island from him for $40,000, a small amount compared to the $170,000 he'd already invested in the park's development.

This left Haymour broke. His wife took their children and left him and as far as he was concerned his life was ruined. He left Canada and vowed revenge. With the help of some cousins, Haymour seized the Canadian Embassy in Beirut and took thirty-four people as hostages. After a nine-hour standoff he was promised he would not be prosecuted for his actions and could return to Canada to settle his disagreement with the provincial government. In the end, Haymour won his case and was awarded $250,000 in compensation. Although he was never given the island back, he did invest the money in nearby Peachland, building an Arabian-themed hotel known as Peachland Castle.

Some might argue this story is far more interesting than having a lake monster live beneath the island, and they'd be right. Truth is often stranger than fiction.

As for the island itself, some people believe it got its name because the island is shaped like a snake or alligator. The terrain is rocky with desert scrub and grass, making it ideal for rattlesnakes to reside there. There were rattlesnakes on the island at one time, but it has been many decades since anyone has confirmed seeing one.

As we approached Squally Point, where Rattlesnake Island sits, Steciuk slowed our vessel down so we could talk. Slowly the island came into view and grew larger. My excitement also grew. I've known about Rattlesnake Island my entire life and seen it in pictures and on television, and even from afar driving south along Highway 97. But I'd never been up close like this.

I looked at Asselin, who is an adventurous sort prone to many days alone in the woods on solo camping trips, and he looked back.

"I want to go on it," he said.

I nodded in response and smiled. "Me too."

Eli overheard our conversation. "You guys are thinking of going on Rattlesnake Island?"

"Yeah," we replied in unison.

Eli turned to Steciuk and asked if it was possible to dock on the island. He said we could circle the island and look, but there's no dock or easy way to beach the boat. If we wanted to go on the island itself, we'd have to swim.

Neither Asselin nor I wore swim wear, but that wasn't a concern. If we got wet, we got wet. How often does one get the chance to venture onto Rattlesnake Island, at least for those of us who don't live in the Okanagan?

Heading to Rattlesnake Island

We drew nearer and the little island loomed larger. It was clear, looking at its rocky shoreline, that it's almost impossible to land a boat there. In fact, we saw a white pole with some kind of light on it, which Steciuk described as a miniature lighthouse.

"It would be easy, if you didn't have proper lights on your boat and were bombing around at night…," I said, letting the thought drift off.

Steciuk agreed, saying a lot of boats have literally run into Rattlesnake Island over the years.

By now, Miller and Ell were on their feet and standing on the edge of our boat, ready to perform a prayer and provide an offering to *N'ha-a-itk*. Eli had his camera ready, but asked permission first, not wanting to cause any offense by filming a sacred ceremony. Miller agreed.

"Alright. It's in a good mood. Let's keep it that way," said Miller.

Truly, aside from a slight breeze causing small ripples across the water, the lake was relatively calm. The sun was warm, and it was an almost perfect day to be on the water. If there is a water spirit, it was most certainly content.

Miller began the prayer in her native language, asking both the water and serpentine spirit's permission for us to be there. She then introduced herself and Ell before making introductions for the rest of us. Then the offering of tobacco was made to the water.

"Thanks for letting us get nice and close to you," Miller said. We were now just metres away from Rattlesnake Island.

"Hang on a sec, guys," said Steciuk.

He powered up the motor, steering us around a submerged outcropping from the island. Had he not, we might have run aground.

The ceremony now over, Eli thanked Miller and Ell for allowing us to film it. We began a slow circle around the island, shooting footage as we went. Eli asked Steciuk about his first expedition to find the Ogopogo in 2000. Steciuk relayed how divers from this adventure swam down eighty feet to explore the caves on the north side of Squally Point.

"The most incredible thing is one of them felt water pressure coming out of one of the caves," said Steciuk.

"Whoa! No kidding!" said Eli.

This suggests something moving inside the cave, be it a current of some sort or, perhaps, *N'ha-a-itk* itself.

Steciuk said Indigenous people in the area believe all the lakes in the region are connected and perhaps these caves are passageways between them.

This set off a little alarm bell in my head, and I'm suddenly back on my windsurf board in the summer of 1998 thinking of the stories my friends and I heard about a monster in Shuswap Lake. So, I spoke up.

"That's the thing we all heard, is that there's a cave that connected (the Shuswap) to Lake Okanagan and people believed it was the same creature passing back and forth between the lakes," I said. "That was back in the late '70s and early '80s that those stories were being passed around out there."

"Yup. Absolutely." Steciuk agreed in his own, laconic way.

"I think every lake, at least in Canada, has a story connected to lake monsters. A similar story," I continued, unable to stop. It was exciting discussing this with open-minded people.

"Oh yeah. Absolutely," said Steciuk, pointing at the lake we travelled on. "This is an immense body of water. It's incredible. It's almost ninety miles long. Three-and-a-half miles across. It's huge!"

Big enough that it's no longer difficult to believe something large could live within it. And, if you believe the theory of these lakes being connected by tunnels, the possibility these creatures exist increases.

I point out how Lake Okanagan and Loch Ness are similar bodies of water and Steciuk agreed, only Lake

Okanagan is bigger. Steciuk said it's actually about four times the size of Loch Ness. Then I mention Ken Gerhard's lake-monster belt, which Steciuk pointed out is an interesting comment.

"It's a little farther north. It's got the same depth, about two hundred to two hundred and twenty (feet deep)," he said. "But it's not as long."

Steciuk and I were really into it, discussing how many of these lakes with monsters alleged to live in them are so similar – right down to the kinds of fish that reside in them and the approximate era each was created. It makes sense stories like the Ogopogo and Nessie would be told, if such creatures exist, that is.

I then realized Asselin and Eli were filming our conversation.

"You know, I'm not a fan of this plesiosaur thing," Steciuk said. I agreed, and I'm secretly so glad Gerhard and I talked before venturing out on this shoot.

"I mean, come on, they died out sixty-five million years ago, and a plesiosaur wasn't a dinosaur anyway," he continued. "It was a reptile."

We're into the description of these monsters now, covering off the similar traits people are seeing all over the world, from the dragon-like head to the serpentine body. Steciuk nodded his head in agreement the entire time. I could tell we're both enjoying this conversation.

He pointed out plesiosaurs were air breathers, which means we'd have a lot more sightings in these lakes if Ogopogo and their like were indeed plesiosaurs.

"I mean they can't hold their breath forever!" Steciuk said.

I mentioned they'd have to be amphibian or mammalian and Steciuk agreed once more.

Steciuk mentioned he's writing a book on Ogopogo and tried to stick with science and reason to come to a conclusion, which he believes he has. Only we'll have to wait and read the book to hear what that is.

This is a book I look forward to reading.

We completed a second circle of the island and decided to venture further into Squally Point itself, which is just south of the island. Steciuk said the area is so named for the way the north and south winds collide along the lake, causing the water to chop and jump or, as such phenomena is referred to nautically, squall.

"Makes sense," said Eli.

I asked Steciuk if the cave systems are located more along Rattlesnake Island or here at Squally Point. He said the caves are located all along this part of the lake. He pointed out that we were in three hundred feet of water, which is amazing given how close to shore we were. This means the land doesn't gently slope out into the lake but goes straight down to the bottom.

"Wow. That's actually pretty nuts," said Eli. "That's actually deeper than Lake Champlain at its deepest."

And this isn't even the deepest part of the lake. Steciuk said that's at the north end near Carrs Landing, one of the many neighbourhoods that border Okanagan Lake.

There the lake is between seven hundred and eight hundred feet.

"And that's only to the sediment," said Steciuk. "Now you've got another twenty-five hundred feet of sediment down to the bottom of the lake."

That makes Lake Okanagan one of the deepest lakes in North America, he said.

"Hence the rumors that it's bottomless," I added.

"Yeah, I guess," Steciuk said, and laughed.

Such talk of Lake Okanagan being a bottomless lake has added fuel to many Ogopogo fans' belief that such a creature could live here. If there is no bottom to the lake, there's lots of room for a family of lake monsters to hide.

"That's wild," said Eli. "It really is just like schism."

Steciuk pointed out that the second deepest part of the lake is near to where we're currently floating, which again makes the area around Rattlesnake Island and Squally Point a good home for *N'ha-a-itk*.

Watson with Rattlesnake Island

We floated in silence for a while before Eli decided it's time to interview Steciuk for the documentary. He prepared his shot, putting Rattlesnake Island firmly in the background, while I switched on my tape recorder. What follows is a transcript of the interview.

Eli took Steciuk back to the beginning, asking what got him interested in the subject of Ogopogo. Steciuk said he wasn't a believer when he moved to Kelowna many, many years ago. But it was that sighting while driving across Okanagan Lake Bridge that convinced him there is a monster living in the lake. This, of course, led to the expeditions where he believes he's had reasonable success in finding evidence that such a creature does exist.

"You've photographed it; am I correct?" Eli asked.

"I've personally seen our friend three times, yes," said Steciuk.

These encounters include the aforementioned one on the bridge and the sonar reading captured during the 2000 expedition. This was returned off Bellevue Creek in the Mission area of Kelowna. This sonar reading suggests a creature some sixty-feet-long was moving through the water.

"And this was just at the end of our three-week expedition. It was quite a long one," said Steciuk.

The third sighting occurred in 2015. Steciuk lives on Lake Okanagan and he and his wife were sitting on their patio facing the lake at about 6:30 at night when something poked its head out of the water.

"Lo and behold our friend stuck his head out of the water and I got an incredible picture. Actually, I got a number of them," he said.

"And I find it rather ironic that all the years I spent in boats floating around the lake looking for Ogopogo here he was right off my patio."

This picture is part of Steciuk's logo for his *Ogopogo Quest* website and adorns T-shirts and mugs that he has for sale. For the record I have one of the mugs, which Steciuk handed out to us at the end of this adventure.

Which brought us to *Ogopogo Quest*. Why did Steciuk launch the site? Simple! The first expedition had drawn enough attention that Steciuk soon found himself inundated with interest in the monster, as well as sightings. It made logical sense to start a public website dedicated to Ogopogo.

"People could call in, report their sightings and keep up on the news of Ogopogo," he said.

The site went live in 2003 and remains a premiere source of Ogopogo sightings and news.

Wanting to get multiple opinions on all things Ogopogo, Eli asked each interviewee the same questions, as well as ones tailored to the individual. When it came time to ask Steciuk about Rattlesnake Island, I was surprised when he hesitated in answering. Several seconds passed before he did.

"I can say Rattlesnake Island is the legendary home of Ogopogo. Certainly, to the First Nations people," he said.

"And, in all honesty there's been a lot of sightings in the area."

He pointed out the very spot where we currently float, with Squally Point to one side of us and Rattlesnake Island to the other, is "an incredible" spot for sightings.

Other than that, he suggested he'd rather have Miller and Ell dive deeper into the relevance of Rattlesnake Island to Ogopogo lore.

Eli continued his questions. Steciuk considers Arlene Gaal one of the greatest Ogopogo researchers in the Okanagan, saying she's gathered more information on the monster than anyone.

"She's known worldwide," he said.

Steciuk kept his answers short and to the point, suggesting that's how he operates. A no-bullshit kind of guy. However, he seemed chattier when the camera wasn't rolling earlier. This is interesting as Steciuk is no stranger to interviews.

When it came to discussing the various theories about what Ogopogo is, he didn't hesitate to share his thoughts. He said a lot of the ideas surrounding Ogopogo are based on preconditioning.

"People have been preconditioned to think you've got a big body of water that's a lake, you've got to have this huge, ancient reptile that lives there. That's not true," he said.

This preconditioning has led to the many theories about the beast's true identity. One theory local to Kelowna is Ogopogo is, in fact, a sturgeon. Sturgeon is the common name for twenty-nine species of fish belonging to the Acipenseridae family. They date back to the Late Cretaceous era and share distinctive characteristics such as a caudal fin like sharks and an elongated, scaleless spindle-like body.

The only problem with that theory is the British Columbian government has publically stated there are no sturgeon in Lake Okanagan, Steciuk said.

"Yes, we do have sturgeon in the Thompson River and the Fraser River, and, because of that, people have thought we have sturgeon there. Ogopogo must be a sturgeon," he said.

"No, I don't think it's a sturgeon."

Steciuk shared his thoughts on Ogopogo being a plesiosaur earlier during our discussion.

On a similar theme, Eli wondered what some of the locals' thoughts and attitudes are about Ogopogo? Do Kelowna residents believe in the monster and what do they think it is? Steciuk said that's an interesting question and, back in 1999, he did a survey asking people one simple question.

"If you saw something in the lake that you couldn't explain, would you call the media and give them your name and your sighting?" he said, repeating the survey question.

Of the thousand people surveyed just eight percent said they would report their sighting. The remaining ninety-two percent would not, said Steciuk.

What he finds most interesting is that if the number of sightings reported during the last twenty-five years represent only eight percent of the actual sightings that occurred, there are plenty more sightings happening than anyone knows about.

"You do the math on that. It's unbelievable," he said.

Ogopogo Quest recently did another survey, this one targeting just two hundred locals. The majority surveyed live on the lake and are about fifty years of age. The same question was asked, and this time twenty-five percent said they'd report a sighting. This suggests to Steciuk that something has changed in terms of people's perception when it comes to Ogopogo.

With science discovering some ten thousand new species of marine life a year, the majority in the world's oceans sure, Steciuk believes minds are opening to the chance that some previously undiscovered species could live in a lake like Lake Okanagan.

What was also interesting about the latest survey is, of the seventy-five percent who said they wouldn't report a sighting, twenty percent of them knew someone who saw something unexplained on the lake themselves and didn't report it.

"So that was quite an interesting survey," Steciuk said.

Based on his statistic, most sightings are reported between August 15 and October 1 and occur south of the bridge towards Squally Point, he said. Once again, this put our little expedition right in a prime Ogopogo sighting location.

As for what people are seeing, the majority come in two forms. One is a whale-like form with appendages, the other a serpentine form. In the serpentine form, the skin is brown or black in color. These sighting put Ogopogo at least thirty-five to forty-feet-long and two-feet-wide.

Steciuk is a wealth of information, I thought, as Eli covered his knowledge of the caves which we discussed off camera for his documentary. I even wondered if it is possible for a creature to travel from lake to lake using these caves.

Miller suddenly spoke up, saying whale bones had been found in Lake Okanagan, which was new information to me but not to Steciuk. The possibility that some form of whale once lived in these waters supports Gerhard's Basilosaurus theories and the sightings of a whale-like creature in the lake.

The whale bones tie into a Westbank First Nations story, which Miller shared with us. Coyote had a twin brother named Fox. Fox and his wife lived together for a long, long time but, one day, the wife became distant to her husband. Then Fox caught his wife making love to someone else… someone who came out of the water.

Fox was upset but decided to wait until later to confront his wife about this infidelity. Instead, he went for a hunt and returned home a time later with meat, only to find his wife was gone.

"Now he's heartbroken," Miller said of Fox.

Fox's brother, Coyote, tried to cheer Fox up. While out and about they saw two maidens travelling down the lake in a canoe. Thinking the maidens might know something about Fox's wife's whereabouts, they hid until the maidens came close.

Suddenly, Fox and Coyote leapt from their hiding spot and Fox demanded to know where his wife was. The maidens said their master had her, but she refused to eat the food provided. The maidens said they ventured out to find food for her to eat.

Coyote killed the maidens and he and Fox put on their clothing and jumped into the canoe. The canoe magically took Fox and Coyote back to the water being's lair. They saw Fox's wife and her suitor, who appeared as a handsome being in person but whose reflection on the water revealed a hideous monster.

Coyote attacked and killed the monster, ripping its head off and tossing it into the coastal water miles away. This is how whales came to be in the ocean. Coyote also proclaimed the being shall never be allowed back in Lake Okanagan.

Whenever she hears stories about Ogopogo having the traits of a whale, she thinks of this legend, said Miller.

"In that story too, that monster's name was *N'ha-a-itk*," she said.

The story is a fascinating one and further adds to the folklore surrounding *N'ha-a-itk* and Ogopogo. I found myself referring to the two incarnations separately in my brain, as the deeper Eli and I dove into this mystery, the clearer it became in my mind that the two versions of the lake monster are distinct.

Ogopogo is the popular product of Western culture and tourism branding by the City of Kelowna. Meanwhile, *N'ha-a-itk* is the original being who settlers and Indigenous people have seen on the lake for centuries. It's the purer version of the two. The one who I believe I was seeking proof of all along.

We decided it was time to turn around and head back to Eldorado, but not before a final pass of Rattlesnake Island. Asselin recorded some drone footage of the island for Eli, and we moved on. Before either of us were aware, we were north of Rattlesnake Island and Asselin and I had missed our opportunity to swim to shore. In the end we shrugged our shoulders, deciding it wasn't meant to be on this trip. We'd be back, we promised ourselves.

My mind was full of ideas. I'd joined Eli in search of a monster I didn't believe existed, at least within the realm of science and Western thinking. In the end I was beginning to believe in a being that wasn't a monster at all but a spirit not unlike the ones Peter Renn and our colleagues at Canadian Paranormal Society went in search of on a regular basis.

Steciuk asked Eli if he's ever piloted a boat like this before, and Eli said he hadn't. So Steciuk turned the controls over to him for the rest of the journey back to the marina. Eli gunned the motor and the increase in velocity blew his trademark black hat off his head.

"Oh no!" he said, turning to grab it but his fingers just missed the brim. Fortunately, I was able to grab the hat before it tumbled into the water; a moment that felt right out of an Indiana Jones movie.

"I'll hold onto it for you," I said.

Eli nodded his thanks.

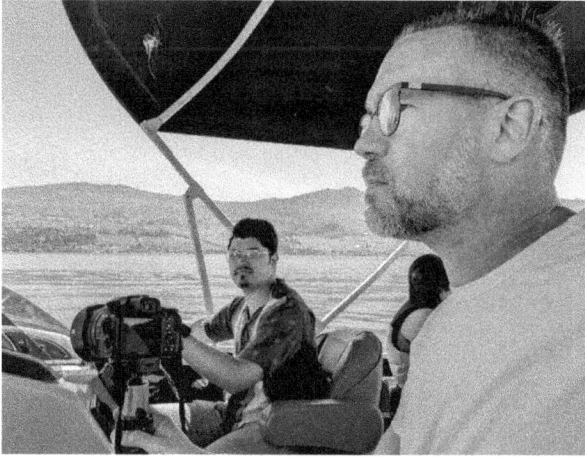
Watson pilots the boat

The rest of the journey back to Eldorado was mostly spent in silence due to the roar of the engine and the wind caused by our rapid cruise across the lake. By the look on Eli's face, he was enjoying his time in the captain's chair but had no qualms turning the controls back to Steciuk for the final approach. Steciuk steered us into the marina and docked us like a pro, which he clearly was after spending so much of his life on the water looking for Ogopogo.

We took our time climbing out of the boat onto the dock. Although we didn't see Ogopogo, I think we all felt like we experienced *N'ha-a-itk* in some way during our voyage. At least Eli and I had, based on conversations to come, but I'll get to that.

Steciuk graciously gave Eli, Miller and I *Ogopogo Quest* mugs adorned with a copy of the picture he had taken from his lakefront home. The image shows… something… poking out of the water. It's blurry, as most images of cryptids are. If he indeed captured the creature's head on film, it looked more like the classic Surgeon's photograph of Nessie than anything else. But that could be a result of the distance Steciuk was from the creature when it surfaced and the need to zoom in on it.

"I didn't realize there would be so many of you, otherwise I would have brought more," Steciuk said, clearly wishing he could have provided mugs for us all. Those who went without assured him they were not offended. We didn't know there would be this many until the day of.

Then it came time for pictures. Eli travelled a long way and, as he put it, Steciuk is a legend in the cryptozoology community. He couldn't travel back to California without getting a picture and Steciuk humbly agreed, dismissing the legend comment.

Yes, I also had my picture taken with Steciuk. How could I not? I'd seen the man on television many times and read several interviews with him about Ogopogo. He was the first interviewee I sought out when putting together an outline for this book. Meeting him and venturing to Rattlesnake Island with him was the thrill of a lifetime.

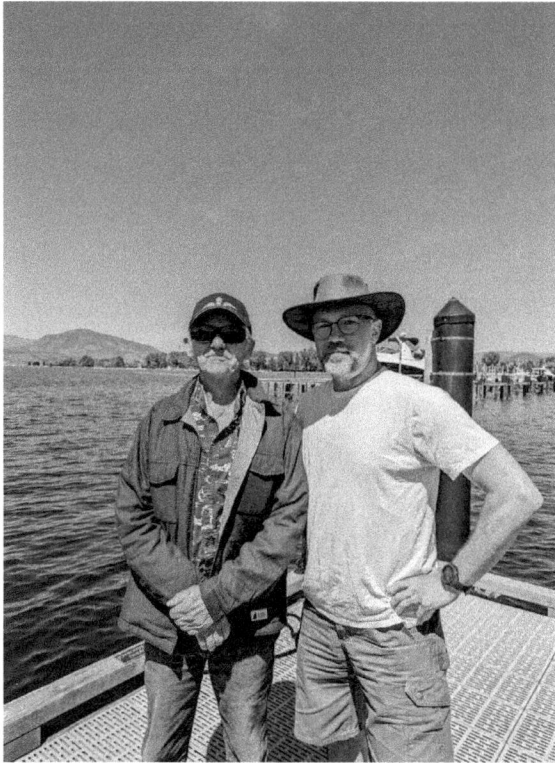
Author with Steciuk

We shook hands with the man and said our goodbyes. Eli covered off the bill for the boat rental, and we made our way back to the truck, promising to deliver Miller and Ell back to the museum.

Asselin set off once we were back at the vehicles, and he and I shared our usual post investigation hug. Eli thanked him for his time and the drone footage, which he compensated Asselin for by giving him a brand-new memory card.

We made it about two blocks when I noticed the parking ticket under my windshield wiper blade. Just as I reached through my open driver's window and snatched it up, a call from Asselin came through on my hands free.

"I got a parking ticket!" he said and laughed.

"It was free parking today. I checked!" I replied, not feeling so full of humor.

But a quick read of the ticket – by Eli, as I was driving – revealed we'd parked against the flow of traffic which, in all my years of driving, I hadn't even realized was a thing. So, my bad. I offered to pay Asselin's fine as well as mine, but he declined, saying he should have known better.

Given this was the only bad thing to happen since our expedition began, I considered myself pretty lucky.

It took about twenty minutes to get Miller and Ell back to the museum. We said our goodbyes and promised to keep in touch. Our conversations had changed my entire thought process about Ogopogo in particular and cryptids in general, and I was thankful for that.

Hungry, we ventured across the parking lot to a Dairy Queen and ordered some burgers and fries. The meal passed in relative silence as Eli checked in with the Small Town Monsters team and I processed my thoughts on the last couple of days; thoughts Eli and I shared on the drive back to our hotel.

"Dude, the more I think about it, the more I think Dale and Colleen really took a picture of Ogopogo," Eli said, summing up my thoughts exactly.

We'd share this sentiment many more times during the remaining twenty-four hours of our adventure.

All the points Hanchar made, made sense to us. The fact the object in the water – the head – didn't bob up and down or move in any way. The long neck disappearing deep into the water. The amazing likeness not only to the statue in the park but to what many witnesses reported seeing for decades. It all added up.

Ditto the water spirit idea. I've written it before in this volume, and I'll do so again here, but it just makes sense. How could a species survive so long in a limited space without a body washing ashore or more sightings taking place? Yes, Lake Okanagan, and other lakes where monsters are sighted, is big but it's still a limited space. The idea this is a living, breathing animal just doesn't make sense.

However, a water spirit that from time to time chooses to make itself known in physical form is worth considering. I've never liked explaining an unknown with another unknown, but given I investigate spirits for a living, and have had experiences to support the notion they exist, I'm not willing to rule out the possibility. In fact, I'm certainly leaning toward it being a very real explanation.

Eli was on the same page. The Bigfoot community, which he is a part of, is divided on the idea of Bigfoot being a paranormal entity and not a missing link. But there is a lot of evidence coming forward supporting the possibility that Bigfoot is something more.

Large footprints in the snow that stop midway through an open field, images depicting a large, ape-like creature taken with thermal imaging cameras that show the figure dissolve into thin air, and sightings of UFOs and strange orbs accompanying Sasquatch sightings are becoming increasingly common.

"It could totally be a water spirit," Eli agreed.

And who are we, as members of Western culture, to say the Indigenous people's beliefs are wrong? We can't, I said. Eli agreed again.

I suggested the last shot of his documentary should be Eli doing as Miller suggested and lifting a cup full of water out of Lake Okanagan. Eli said he would think about it.

A Few Loose Ends

Back at the hotel, we retreated to our separate rooms for a bit of relaxation before meeting with Laurie Gaal. I was restless though after two very busy days and overwhelmed with the degree of information Eli and I had recorded. There was also the matter of two interviews to prepare for. One for the very documentary I was a part of, as Eli wanted to include me among the interviews. The other was for the Small Town Monsters documentary currently filming in Harrison Hot Springs. I was to go from Ogopogo to Bigfoot and speak intelligently on both subjects. Suffice to say, I was a little nervous.

My phone pinged and it was time to meet with Gaal. She'd agreed to meet us at a nearby Starbucks a short ten-minute drive away. Gaal did not agree to be filmed or formally interviewed for the documentary, so I don't feel comfortable transcribing the conversation for this book. I will, however, paraphrase the meeting as best I can.

Eli wanted to meet Gaal to discuss purchasing the rights to use the Folden Film in the documentary. Gaal's mother, Arlene, owned the only copy of the film and it remained among her collection when she died. Sure, there's various copies floating around online, but Eli wanted to use the real film.

Gaal was honest with us; she hadn't had time to sift through her mother's extensive catalogue of Ogopogo sightings, films, books, and other related paraphernalia. She wanted to do so with the help of her brother, who is overseas, and the global pandemic prevented him from coming home and helping.

The good news is he was scheduled to arrive in Kelowna within the next couple of weeks and they would start going through her mother's Ogopogo material then, along with her other belongings. She would be able to provide Eli with an answer on use of the Folden Film once that was done.

Eli hadn't received word on whether he could use the original film at the time of this writing and was considering using a copy of the Folden footage in this documentary.

A big part of our discussion revolved around what would happen to Arlene's Ogopogo research material. Eli and I are both aware of cases where an investigator's children have simply tossed the life's work into the trash, the material lost forever. Our hope was that would not be the case with Arlene's vast collection. Gaal told us she hadn't given it much thought yet, and Eli and I implored her not to get rid of it. Donate it to a museum, sell it to another Ogopogo researcher, or even let us purchase it. The material is too valuable to the field of cryptozoology to have it lost forever.

We could tell she admired our enthusiasm and promised she would not toss the research away.

That is pretty much the gist of our conversation. Gaal seemed a bit nervous to meet us but warmed to our company once we got talking. She'd been approached by many

Ogopogo enthusiasts and researchers about her mother and her mother's work and seemed a bit overwhelmed by it all. Hopefully our laidback demeanors helped put her at ease.

With that, the conversation ended and Gaal said her goodbyes. Eli and I decided it was time to head back to the hotel and complete my interview. My heart leapt into my throat. Even though I knew it was coming and had spent weeks cramming every bit of Ogopogo history and information into my brain, I was nervous to be interviewed on camera. As a former journalist and broadcaster, I was used to asking the questions, not having them asked of me.

Eli decided to film the interview in my hotel room and made a few furniture adjustments to make the environment look more scholarly. It's amazing what moving a lamp and adding a few books to a desk can do. I won't bore you with the details of the interview as Eli asked the same questions of me as he did the other interviewees, adding a few more personal points as I had become as much a part of this adventure as he was. About ten to fifteen minutes later we were done.

"That was great dude," Eli said. I took his word for it.

While returning the hotel room to its usual state Eli turned to me and said, "You know, I am going to use your suggestion and make the last shot of the documentary me filling up a cup of water in the lake."

"Yeah?" I felt proud that he liked my idea.

"Yeah. That'll sum everything up nicely and make for a good ending."

"Awesome. Thanks, man."

"Thank you, dude."

The hotel room back in order we decided to head to a beach and record the final shot of the documentary before we grabbed a concluding dinner in Kelowna. We decided to film at a beach enroute to Eldorado as Eli liked the look of it. We'd capture the setting sun as well. So off we went, grabbing a couple of the hotel's plastic glasses on the way out the door. Ten minutes later we pulled into a parking lot close to the beach.

The sun was a bright yellowish orange and the sky perfectly clear. Light danced across the water while swimmers splashed about, finding refuge from the unusually hot May weather. The way the light played about it wasn't hard to believe that *N'ha-a-itk* was in a good mood as evening approached.

To my surprise Eli wanted to include me in the conclusion, so he instructed me to take a glass, walk down to the lake, fill the glass with water, and hold it up in front of me, as if toasting the lake. I did as directed, and Eli followed me with the camera to capture the moment.

"Dude, that looked great!" Eli said.

"Thanks, man!"

He handed me the camera, saying we'd repeat the shot only with me filming him. So, I hefted the camera, hit record on Eli's command, and began filming what would be the final shot of the documentary. I followed Eli to the lake, focusing on his hand as he scooped the cup into the water and rose with it as he hefted it before him.

Then I took some initiative and moved behind Eli, changing the frame on his face from left to right so the setting sun shone brightly at him, making it look like he was gazing toward new beginnings.

Or at least that's what I thought.

"And cut," Eli said, turning to me. "How'd it look?"

I handed him the camera. "Take a look."

He played back the footage and smiled. "Dude, that looks sick!"

"Thank you!"

Eli was visibly excited by how the conclusion to his documentary turned out. He seemed particularly pleased with my footage of him.

We walked back to the truck and decided sushi would make a nice final meal in Kelowna. We drove to a nearby restaurant and soon found ourselves enjoying some raw fish and rice.

Walking back to the truck I received a phone call from my son. His evening good-night call. I was relieved when he told me he had one more baby tooth to come out, so I actually hadn't missed being present for that final visit from the Tooth Fairy!

"I'll see you in two nights, pal. I love you."

"Love you too, Dad!"

We hung up and I told Eli the good news about Griffon's tooth. He smiled.

"Right on, man."

Back to the hotel we went, meeting outside after a quick clean up for a few final drinks for me and puff on the pipe for Eli before we called it a night. We had a 6:30 wake up the next morning so I could get Eli to the Small Town Monsters shoot in Harrison, and I had an interview about Bigfoot awaiting me as well.

Eli and I had one more interview to record on Ogopogo, this time with former police officer and cryptozoologist John Kirk.

No rest for the wicked.

Get On with the Job

Six thirty came way too early but somehow, I managed to rise, shower, take care of my morning business and get dressed all within about fifteen minutes. Eli and I were on the road south to British Columbia's Lower Mainland by seven.

We passed the time talking music and movies, and Eli took in the view, which includes the majestic Cascade Mountains that jut up into the sky and almost always have a bit of snow at the peaks. Eli said they remind him of the mountains in Alaska. I took his word for it, having never been.

We were scheduled to meet his Small Town Monsters companions at a bed and breakfast in Chilliwack, a city of more than eighty thousand people that's about thirty minutes south of Harrison Hot Springs. My grandparents lived in Chilliwack while I was growing up, so I've spent a lot of time there in my youth, and my wife and son like to frequent the neighbourhood of Cultus Lake, which is a lakeside resort area.

The film crew rented their headquarters in a rural area to the north of the city, a part of Chilliwack I'd never been to before. The long, straight roads and wide-open fields – Chilliwack is known for its corn harvest – were new to me and I enjoyed taking in the view as much as Eli.

Thankfully, Google Maps navigated us to our destination with little confusion, and we were soon parked and shaking hands with the Small Town Monsters team. There wasn't a lot of time for idle chitchat though as Seth Breedlove and company quickly whisked Eli away to film a sequence for the Bigfoot film. I stayed behind with researcher/producer Heather Moser, cinematographer Zac Palmisano and interviewer Mark Matzke and recorded my interview about Sasquatch.

That task complete, I enjoyed a fun afternoon hanging out with Moser, Palmisano and Matzke. We drank coffee and talked the paranormal and filmmaking and what got us involved in this fascinating subject. Matzke and I share a love of all things Godzilla, so he and I bonded over many talks about the famous Toho monster. By the time the afternoon was over, and Eli returned, I believed I had made three new friends.

But one last Ogopogo-themed interview remained. I had reached out to John Kirk, one of the co-founders, and current chairman, of the British Columbia Scientific Cryptozoology Club and asked to interview him for this book. A former member of our Royal Canadian Mounted Police, Kirk is a leading investigator and researcher on the subject of Bigfoot, lake monsters, and other cryptids and has authored a book about Ogopogo. I didn't actually get to speak with him, as the interview was shot down by one of his colleagues due to me being a paranormal investigator.

However, both Breedlove and Eli were able to secure interviews with Kirk for their respective documentaries, and

Eli encouraged me to be a part of his and use the material for this book. Once Kirk's Bigfoot interview was complete, he sat down with us for our final interview on the subject of Ogopogo. What follows is a transcript of the interview.

Looking more like a biker than a scientific researcher, Kirk is quick to point out that he uses tools and techniques that he honed during his years as a policeman to secure possible evidence of cryptids. The hope is these unknown creatures will one day be officially catalogued by science, he said.

"My whole reason for being involved in this field was an act of fate that I will never forget," Kirk said in response to Eli's question about what got him interested in Ogopogo.

Kirk moved to Canada from Hong Kong in 1987. On May 19 of that year, he and his then wife travelled to Kelowna hoping to connect with his wife's friend. The only clue they had is this friend owned a winery. While seeking out information on the friend, Kirk noticed his son and another travelling companion were arguing, which seemed unusual to Kirk as his son rarely argued with anyone about anything.

"This must have incensed him. I'm going to find out what's made him so annoyed," said Kirk, reflecting back.

Kirk said he approached his son and asked him what the matter was.

"She keeps saying that's a boat," the son said, and pointed at an object out in the lake. "And I'm telling you that's not a boat. That's a head."

What Kirk saw was indeed a head, and a big one at that given how far away from it the trio were. He said it was easily two to three-feet-long and glided along the lake's surface at a decent clip.

"Without making any wake," he added. "No bow wake. No trailing wake. Nothing."

Whatever it was turned from its southward course and headed east across the lake. Kirk eventually lost sight of the object but had no doubt in his mind he'd just witnessed the thing people call Ogopogo.

Fifteen to twenty minutes later Kirk and company heard dogs barking nearby. Kirk said he first looked at the dogs, then turned his gaze to what had riled them up. There, floating in the lake, was a sixty-foot-long creature with a small head, long neck and five or six humps behind it. Beneath the surface was what must have been a tail.

"And I'm looking at this thing and I can't believe my eyes that there's something that big in the lake," said Kirk.

Kirk had his Hi-8 video camera and began filming the object. Suddenly it sunk vertically down into the lake's depths, much like a submarine will do when diving. A slick of what might have been body oils was left behind on the surface in the shape of what had been lying there.

"It was astonishing. Some people said, 'What you saw was cloud shadow'. Cloud shadow doesn't leave an oily slick. Organic material does," said Kirk.

"I'm thinking to myself 'We've seen this thing twice in a day, so it's real. What is it?'"

Why hasn't anyone identified this creature scientifically, Kirk wondered to himself. He believes the monster's association to First Nations' folklore prompted most serious researchers to dismiss the subject. He referred to this as a "colonialist mindset."

"Which is rubbish. Native people don't make up stuff. They don't have supernatural creatures that are different from animals we know," he said, adding Indigenous people refer to ravens, crows, wolves, bears and other animals as having supernatural abilities.

"They are all based on animals that are known in the complex organic world."

Kirk is well versed in the Westbank First Nations' beliefs surrounding *N'ha-a-itk*/Ogopogo, saying they were "ten miles ahead of the Neo-Colonialists" when it came to acknowledging the creature's existence.

"We needed to find out what this animal was, and I made a conscious decision that I would not rest until I found out what it really is," he said.

Kirk acknowledges May 19 every year, saying that day back in 1987 brought him out of his comfort zone. Used to dealing with hard facts and evidence as a police officer and in his dealing with journalists, he knew investigating this lake monster required him to do the same and work with like-minded people, especially if he was going to launch a major expedition to do it.

He found James Clark, a freelance writer, and Pal Leblond, the then head of the oceanography department at the University of British Columbia. Both men were interested in starting a cryptozoology club and Kirk knew he had to be a part of that. The club became the British Columbia Scientific Cryptozoology Club. The club is now in its thirty-fourth year.

The group has faced its share of mockery and cynicism from people who don't understand what the club is trying to do, said Kirk. These cynics seem to think Kirk and company are seeking some supernatural beast, but he maintains that's not the case. Ogopogo and other cryptids are flesh-and-blood creatures that haven't been scientifically identified yet.

"We need to figure out what the heck this thing is. That's been sort of a life pursuit for me," he said.

What makes Lake Okanagan unique in Kirk's mind is that it's a deep glacial lake – up to a thousand feet deep in two places – with an outlet at the south end of the lake that becomes the Okanagan River. The river connects to Skaha Lake, Vaseux Lake and ultimately Osoyoos Lake, creating a vast network for aquatic life to easily travel between the three lakes. Within these waters is vast tonnage of fish, shrimp, and other marine life for an animal like Ogopogo to feed on.

He recalled a time in 1989 when he and Clark were on a boat just off Rattlesnake Island. Clark tapped Kirk on the shoulder and said, "You better take a look at this."

Kirk looked into the water and saw thousands of half-digested shrimps floating on the surface in an oily slick.

"It's like something puked it up," Kirk said.

Clark scooped up the shrimp and the oily liquid, and the men took the sample to Lablond so it could be tested at one of the university's labs. Sadly, the sample was lost.

"There was no chain of custody, no preparation of a filing system for it and we lost that," he said. "That was an ideal opportunity to find out what it was because DNA could have been obtained from that."

Like many lakes worldwide Lake Okanagan faces an environmental challenge due to the humans who live, work, and play in and around the water. There's sewage, oil slicks from recreational boats, as well as garbage people carelessly dump in the water. Kirk said residents are trying to do right by the lake, and efforts to keep it clean are improving, but he believes it's imperative the lake is protected, not only for residents but this mysterious species that lives within it as well.

He pointed out it was his organization that was instrumental in efforts to get Ogopogo protected under the British Columbia Wildlife Act, which occurred in the late 1980s.

Kirk refuted claims that Ogopogo could reside in an underwater cave near Rattlesnake Island and Squally Point. In 1989 he was joined by Chris Roper of Robotic Systems International, and they scoured the submerged portion of the island with a robotic underwater camera. He's since been back with Japanese and French film crews to do the same and each time has found nothing resembling such a cave system, he said.

Which I find interesting given what Steciuk has told us about his dive team's experiences with caves near Rattlesnake Island. Kirk said there are fissures big enough for something like an eel to hide in, but not something the size of Ogopogo.

"You're talking about an animal that could be sixty to seventy feet long in the ultra-adult stage and there's absolutely no way that it could be there," he said.

He continued, saying some Okanagan natives believe Rattlesnake Island is the home of *N'ha-a-itk* or Ogopogo, but not all Indigenous stories are united on that front. These deviations include the origin of the creature itself.

As far as Kirk is concerned when it comes to Ogopogo, the relevance of Squally Point and Rattlesnake Island is strictly based in folklore. He's come to this conclusion tracking the numerous sightings over the years, adding there are sightings in that part of the lake, but the creature has been seen on all parts of the lake, no one area more than any other.

Eli asked Kirk about his thoughts on some key Ogopogo researchers, including Arlene Gaal and Bill Steciuk. He said Arlene Gaal was and is still referred to as "The Lady of the Lake" due to her enthusiasm and knowledge of the subject.

"She was a really enthusiastic investigator/researcher," he said, adding he didn't always see eye to eye with her but always respected her.

The biggest point he and Gaal disagreed on was a piece of footage referred to in Ogopogo lore as the Chaplin

Footage. On July 18, 1989, a car salesman from Kelowna captured footage of a thirteen-foot-long creature flicking its tail in the lake.

I can remember the excitement this footage generated back in the day, especially because the long-running TV series *Unsolved Mysteries* purchased the rights to Ken Chaplin's film. The first time most people were able to see it was when it broadcast on an episode of the show. Stills from the video were also sold to the various tabloid newspapers of the day.

Chaplin claimed the footage he captured was of Ogopogo and Gaal agreed. Kirk and many others believe it was actually a mammal, probably a beaver or river otter.

"No gigantic creature can flick its tail that quickly," he said. "You would have heard an explosion when that tail hit the water and all you heard was a flap."

I'm inclined to side with Kirk and company on this one. My dad and I watched that episode of *Unsolved Mysteries* and both of us exclaimed "That's not Ogopogo. That's a beaver!" when we saw the animal flick its tail in the footage.

Kirk believes the Folden Film is a legitimate bit of Ogopogo footage, however he disagreed on Gaal and others' assessment of the creature's size. Many believe it to be sixty or seventy feet in length, but Kirk is convinced it's more like forty-feet-long.

He backs this up saying he and members of the *Skeptical Inquirer* investigated the point where the footage was filmed and took laser measurements of the landscape et cetera. The skeptics believed it to be smaller than thirty feet, which Kirk disagreed with as well because of the size of the bow wake the creature creates moving through the water.

"You always have to have skeptics. If you don't have skeptics, you're a believer and belief is a useless emotion and sentiment," he said. "It's a balanced scientific perspective and if you have respectful decent conversations with skeptics you come to conclusions."

As for Steciuk, Kirk said the two men have shared a mutual respect for two decades now, largely because Steciuk also approaches the subject matter from a scientific point of view, using sonar and other modern technologies to search the lake.

"Bill has been very diligent. His search methods are second to none. I really like the guy," said Kirk. "His work is there to be respected and admired."

Kirk has done a lot of his own research into and exploration for Ogopogo since that May day in 1987, applying science to a subject scientists tend to dismiss. Is it a mammal, reptile or amphibian? He's ruled out reptile for many of the same reasons Gerhard has.

"This thing is either a mammal or an amphibian. That's where the dilemma exists now. It's got features of both," said Kirk.

"This is a curiosity that is so odd and so strange. It doesn't seem to fit comfortably into any niche, so we need to get on with the job."

Getting on with the job has meant hundreds of hours searching Lake Okanagan on various expeditions, both on his own and with other club members. He even took part in the Nippon TV expedition in 1991.

It was during that expedition that the pilot of a deep rover descended to the lake bottom and immediately saw something "take off" and leave a massive spray of silt in its wake, Kirk said.

"We've used sonar, underwater cameras. We've had divers down there with cameras in addition to the robot cameras and we've done so much sighting observation and been blessed with a whole bunch of sightings," he said.

Despite all this effort they have yet to capture any conclusive footage of the monster in Lake Okanagan. Kirk believes the Folden Film is the most conclusive bit of film taken of Ogopogo because it reveals "a giant something" living in the lake.

"It isn't a fish. There's no fish in Okanagan Lake that's remotely near how big that thing is. Even if it was twelve-feet-long there's no fish in Okanagan Lake that's twelve-feet-long," said Kirk.

"By process of elimination you realize there's an animal of inordinate size living in that lake, and you need to get on with the job."

Kirk has been getting on with the job for more than thirty years now and, although he does become frustrated at times – more with some of the people he's had to work with than the elusive Ogopogo or efforts to find it – he never tires of it.

In fact, he was scheduled to return to Kelowna not long after the conclusion of this interview. However, this trip was more for pleasure than a full-on search for the animal living in the lake.

"This time I'm going to sit there and drink beer and eat – at waterside sites. I'm not going to do what I usually do which is sit there with cameras and binoculars and telescopes and recording equipment and all that jazz," he said.

Why?

"That thing shows up every time I'm not expecting it so going out there and thinking you're going to see it and having all that equipment around is hit and miss."

Although any hard evidence of Ogopogo's existence remains inconclusive, Kirk is sure of one thing: a lot of people have seen something out on Lake Okanagan that has four or five humps that's anywhere between ten- and seventy-feet-long and has a head like a horse, camel, or sheep. The descriptions are similar enough.

With that, the interview draws to a close.

The next few hours were spent mingling with the Small Town Monsters crew and joining them for dinner in nearby Harrison Hot Springs. Getting to know people whose work I've enjoyed and admired for years. Finding them to be genuinely good people was a highlight of the year for me for sure.

After saying goodbye to Eli, and both of us promising to keep in touch, I checked in to a nearby hotel for the night and experienced a tired that I hadn't felt before. The last three days were nonstop, and I realized I was running on adrenalin. Now that it was all over, I was crashing hard and thankful I wasn't attempting to drive back to Kamloops this same night.

But what an adventure it was!

Final Thoughts

Months later the events of those three May days and the interviews and research that proceeded it still swirl in my brain. Is Ogopogo real, and, if so, what is it? Does my belief that lake monsters can't possibly exist hold up?

I'm now inclined to agree with John Kirk on the subject of belief, but not in the way he intended it. I can no longer believe that lake monsters DO NOT exist. All the interviews undertaken for this book, my time spent with witnesses, and Eli's and my adventures in Kelowna have convinced me there is something living in Lake Okanagan. If something is living in that lake, the same is possible in other lakes where monsters are reported.

Did Hanchar and Hanson capture this monster on camera that October day in 2022? Eli and I are convinced they did. Skeptics say it was a swimming dog or duck. John Kirk thinks it's a rotting crawfish. But Eli and I did our due diligence, compared images of these claims to the picture, and disagree. The creature they took a picture of matches the description of what people have been seeing in that lake for hundreds, if not thousands, of years and closely resembles the statue in Kelowna's park.

Then what is Ogopogo? Is it a flesh-and-blood creature like Ken Gerhard and John Kirk believe? Or is it a water spirit like Coralee Miller and other Indigenous people believe? Again, Eli and I lean more toward the spiritual than physical. I've said many times that I don't like explaining an unknown with another unknown, but I've had spiritual experiences that have convinced me life after death is possible and ghosts – whatever they are – are around us all the time. Then why can't there be a spirit inhabiting a body of water? Who's to say Western science and medicine is right and aboriginal belief is wrong? I can't. Talking with Miller and other First Nations has swayed my thinking.

There is something in Okanagan Lake and other lakes in Ken Gerhard's lake-monster belt. But I don't think it's what most cryptozoologists believe it is. I think it's something beyond our physical world and understanding and is something not to be feared but respected. If you respect it, it will respect you in return.

So, the next time you visit Okanagan Lake – or even Loch Ness or Lake Champlain – walk down to the shore with a cup or glass in hand and dip it into the water. Do so and you'll encounter the creature that dwells within those waters.

Just remember to pour the water back into the lake before you leave.

Author and Watson in Kelowna at Soelin Ogopogo statue